AYAHUASCA

Sacred Plant Medicines, Healing
& Psychedelic Experiences

SOFIA VISCONTI

© Copyright 2022 - All rights reserved.

The content contained within this book may not be reproduced, duplicated, or transmitted without direct written permission from the author or the publisher.

Under no circumstances will any blame or legal responsibility be held against the publisher, or author, for any damages, reparation, or monetary loss due to the information contained within this book, either directly or indirectly.

Legal Notice:

This book is copyright protected. It is only for personal use. You cannot amend, distribute, sell, use, quote, or paraphrase any part, or the content within this book, without the consent of the author or publisher.

Disclaimer Notice:

Please note the information contained within this document is for educational and entertainment purposes only. All effort has been executed to present accurate, up-to-date, reliable, complete information. No warranties of any kind are declared or implied. Readers acknowledge that the author is not engaged in the rendering of legal, financial, medical, or professional advice. The content within this book has been derived from various sources. Please consult a licensed professional before attempting any techniques outlined in this book.

By reading this document, the reader agrees that under no circumstances is the author responsible for any losses, direct or indirect, that are incurred as a result of the use of the information contained within this document, including, but not limited to, errors, omissions, or inaccuracies.

SUBSCRIBE TO
SOFIA VSICONTI

Greetings!

As a subscriber, you will receive a **Free Gift +** You will be the first to hear about new books, articles and more exclusives **just for you.**

Simply scan the QR code to join.

CONTENTS

IMPORTANT INFORMATION 1

INTRODUCTION 5
- VINE OF THE ANCESTORS 6
- WHAT IS IT? 8
- YEAH, BUT WHAT *IS* IT…? 10
- DRUGS, PSYCHEDELICS, AND TRYPTAMINES 15
- AYAHUASCA VS OTHER TRYPTAMINE PSYCHEDELICS 20

CHAPTER 1: PSYCHEDELIC PHYSIOLOGY 29
- IT'S ALREADY THERE 30
- WHAT AYAHUASCA DOES IN THE BRAIN 32
- WHAT AYAHUASCA DOES IN THE BODY 34
- IS IT REAL? 36
- WHAT DOES IT MEAN? 40

CHAPTER 2: ENTHEOGENIC MEDICINE 47
- MEDICINE. SORT OF. 47
- DEPRESSION 52
- ADDICTION 55
- POST-TRAUMATIC STRESS DISORDER 56
- NEUROGENESIS AND NEUROPLASTICITY 59

CHAPTER 3: SHAMANISM 63
- BELIEF BEFORE RELIGION 64
- PRANKSTERS, CHARLATANS, AND AYAHUASCEROS 67
- THE MYSTERY OF THE MIXTURE 73

CHAPTER 4: TAKING AYAHUASCA 77
- THE RISKS 79
- TYRAMINE POISONING 81
- THE SPACE 83
- THE DOSE 87

Drinking 89
  Taking Off 90
  Being Elsewhere 91
  Peaking 93
  Riding It 95
  Returning 97
  Coming Back to Baseline 99
  Afterwards 101

CHAPTER 5: PSYCHEDELIC EXPLORATION 103
  Intrepidation 104
  Psychedelic Culture 109
  Ayahuasca Tourism 114
  Microdosing 117

CHAPTER 6: THE PSYCHEDELIC LIFESTYLE 121
  Should You Try Ayahuasca? 121
  Getting a Supply 124
  Ayahuasca Groups 128
  Ayahuasca and Teenagers 130

AYAHUASCA AND THE FREE CITIZEN 137

CONCLUSION 139
  Set Out 141

REFERENCES 145

OTHER BOOKS BY SOFIA VISCONTI 151

IMPORTANT INFORMATION

This is not a book about drugs. This is a book about the exploration of the human mind, where the use of certain plants forms one part of the process. This book does not explicitly advocate the use of Ayahuasca, but it does advocate informed exploration free from the corrupting effects of failing to separate intelligent use from criminal abuse.

In almost every country, Ayahuasca is illegal for personal use, and it is also illegal under the UN Convention on Psychotropic Substances which outlaws it as being of such a risk to society it needs international control. The constituent plants it is made from are not outlawed but extract some of the psychoactive ingredients, mix them together, and take or sell them and you will be breaking the laws in most countries. In the few countries where it is legal, trafficking it out is still a criminal offense.

Ayahuasca related cases are regularly prosecuted around the world, though convictions are inconsistent but can be serious when they are made.

All drugs have a psychological and physical impact,

and what goes up, must come down. Each person has their own sensitivities and appetite for these things, with psychedelics, in particular, having associations with mental illness. Most of the alarming stories are untrue or misrepresented, but there is no denying that underlying mental health issues and psychedelics can bring unpredictable results. Anyone considering using Ayahuasca must consider the bigger picture of their mental health.

The contents of this book are educational and presented so the reader can make their own opinions. This book is not exhaustive and presents only one perspective on Ayahuasca, and the potential user is encouraged to research and cross-reference other sources. Some details have been omitted or are intentionally vague, either due to the legal implications, the amount of data being beyond the scope of this book, or in most cases both.

Psychedelic drugs have a substantial history with scientific research and we don't intend to divert from that. This book presents science, as peer-reviewed research, socio-anthropological observation, and self-aware anecdotes. Select references are included, though the identities of those providing anecdotal content have in some cases been omitted. Material that makes claims of a religious or spiritual nature has been kept to a minimum but is amply covered elsewhere.

Ayahuasca is not a toy or novelty, the effects are

intense, serious, and engaging. Anyone who uses Ayahuasca or any other drug based on the contents and opinions of this book is, in the ethics of psychedelic exploration, presumed to be self-determined, self-confident, self-directed, and self-selected, otherwise they should abstain.

INTRODUCTION

There's more to the world and we all know it, and our species has spent much of its history trying to catch glimpses of it. Sometimes we do, and sometimes we just think we do, and entire cultures and civilizations have evolved with these things at their core.

You are sitting and reading this right now in a culture orchestrated by the religions, ideologies, philosophies, and practices of its past. You could be in Toronto or Tokyo, Tehran or Nairobi, and the shape of your experience is defined by what your culture thinks all this means.

For many, this questioning is seen as someone else's job, either someone else back in history or someone too important for you to meet. Few people see themselves in the driving seat of delving into the meaning and machinations of reality, either content that it doesn't affect them or quietly but painfully aware they don't know.

But it isn't always like this.

Methods and processes exist where anyone can take their "culture goggles" off and experience things with the trappings of consensual reality removed, and have not just a glimpse of the realities behind this one, but immerse themselves in it. Unlike other methods such as the various yogas, trances, internal states, and extreme ordeals, this family of methods is both reliable and even fun.

Until the turn of the millennium, not a lot of people had heard of ayahuasca, and still, the number of people who heard of it far outweighs the number who have actually done it, with a lot of information going about being low quality, if not inexperienced plagiarism.

Ayahuasca was jumped on quickly by all manner of charlatans, self-anointed gurus, trendsetters, and hucksters, selling it as a remedy for all things just as they had goji berries, waterbeds, colonic irrigation, and macrobiotics in the past. Thanks to the emergence of the podcast as a major source of infotainment.

Vine of the Ancestors

Ayahuasca goes by several names, in several languages, and by different tribes to denote what it means to them. This is not surprising considering the number of languages of the Amazon area, further split by modern countries and the intrusion of European languages. Multiple names exist for the same thing within the same language, depending on use, part, age, and process.

"Ayahuasca" itself is a Latinized spelling of a Quechuan word, combining the words for the spirit of a dead person (Aya) and rope or vine (Huasca). Most names refer to the vine, Banisteriopsis Caapi in botanical nomenclature, with this botanical term itself referring to Kapi, one of many names for the vine across several languages.

Ayahuasca is often abbreviated to mean simply vine, or in the case of some modern groups, the nickname Aya. Local groups can call the prepared brew a wide spectrum of names including Nichi, Mihi, and simply Vegi meaning plant, though this can include the additives of other things ranging from perfumes to other drugs like Datura.

A common name is Yaje, the name it first came to popular modern attention by, following the reports of western researchers and explorers, including writer William Burroughs, who published an account and discussed it using the name. Another common name is Daime or Damiane, which has a Christian connotation but also refers to the name of other plants that are smoked or drunk ceremonially, not necessarily with psychedelic properties.

The other half of the mix, Psychotria Viridis, is much more humble despite it containing the tryptamine DMT and is usually called Chakruna or Chakria, also Quechuan words.

Here we use the name *Ayahuasca* for the sake of continuity, to mean the traditional concoction or a close version to it prepared the same way. We use the term with respect for the traditions it comes from, but not necessarily when used the same way, including the literal translation that it implies dealing with passed ancestors.

What Is It?

Ayahuasca is a concoction of two Amazonian plants that when brewed and drunk, initiate a profound psychedelic experience that lasts about five hours. Over centuries, this experience has been explored and refined by cultures of the Amazon forests, so it can be navigated and employed for a range of personal and social reasons.

The experience is overwhelmingly unusual, and unlike almost any other drug, it is deeply social in nature, very safe, and has positive results. Unlike other drugs, even closely related ones, Ayahuasca does not leave you reeling and in a low state, returning you to normal or even refreshed.

This experience never actually changes you as a person. You don't feel drunk or euphoric, stimulated, inebriated, or stoned, it just changes what you are perceiving. None of your faculties for critical thinking or reasoning or engaging change, making it impossible to dismiss it all as the distortions of a disrupted mind.

In the eyes of most modern states, Ayahuasca *as a drug* is outlawed, usually classed in the highest order of control with drugs deemed of no value to society, but plants containing the ingredients are often unrestricted. Unlike most drugs, Ayahuasca does not take a complex and involved process of extraction and production, being able to be turned from raw plant matter into an active concoction by anyone with a fire or stove.

Most of its use is traditional or as a recreation and adaptation of this, very rarely being known as a party or recreational thing. The effects do not lend themselves to high-energy dancing and environments, seemingly naturally being intimate, contemplative, or esoteric. Due to this, users don't represent any stereotypical drug culture, though there is music, art, literature, and certain life choices that go with it, none of which align with the extensive illegal drug industrial complex.

It comes as untreated plant matter, no more unusual than what you sweep up from your garden, as chunks of the thick vine and leaves much like anything you'll see in the herb aisle. Even the commercially powdered versions are no more unusual than things like cinnamon or green tea, and certainly less exotic than much of which is found in traditional medicine from China.

For the rich psychedelic world it unfurls, Ayahuasca requires little of you from this world, and though some groups exist as churches, that's certainly not necessary either for supply or support. In traditional use it is usually used casually with much less ritual than some expect, often being about as formal as a yoga session and in some cases no more ceremonial than having coffee.

Surprisingly perhaps, is that Ayahuasca is identified with the beta-carboline source, not the DMT one, perhaps because it is independently active to a fairly mild degree. This suggests the Banisteriopsis Caapi vine was known as a psychoactive but the Psychotria leaf was not because the DMT couldn't be initiated, which hints at the magical quality that the radical Ayahuasca effect has. To people with no other way of knowing, the Psychotria leaf has no special properties until mixed with the vine where it turns a weird tea into a full-blown psychedelic experience.

Yeah, But What *Is* It...?

As easy as it is to understand Ayahuasca at a chemical, botanical, and cultural level, what it is in the greater picture of intelligent life on an evolving planet is a whole other thing. We understand plants have endogenous chemicals that act as pesticides and ways of advantage for propagation, but we don't know why some have chemicals that mimic the human brain at its most dynamic.

Theories about this get fanciful fast, going from evolutionary happenstance to extraterrestrial life in only one or two leaps, and either way, having an extremely broad view that is bigger than simply finding a natural pesticide that gets you high. At its most simplistic, Ayahuasca is a mix that opens a human cultural door that connects to different perceptions and the experience around that.

Chance? Maybe, but it would be an anomaly to have something with no other perceptible function when so many other functional ones exit. Plus, evolution tends not to work that way, and though based on random mutation, the uptake of these is not by chance, with the things that carry on doing so because they have advantages in a certain ecological niche.

A common description of Ayahuasca, and especially DMT, is that it's a door into another universe like it's some kind of science fiction thing. This isn't quite as trite as it sounds if you consider that another universe would have different physical and chronological laws by which the things in it happened in different ways for different reasons, by which metric Ayahuasca starts to qualify, minus the high future-tech space stuff.

Research has long been stuck trying to explain this, that out of the tens of millions of plant species, the combination of two that mimic human neurology was found, processed, and found to be safe. This assumes that human evolution has been driven by random opportunism.

Whenever Ayahuasca has arrived at it, it was by modern humans, with the same brains and capacity for intelligence that we have today. Although theories exist for the use of psychedelics among our ancestors, this is not what happened in the Amazon, where people arrived with brains as we have right now. We don't know the extent to which a taste for psychedelics traveled with us from the old world, nor how the combination for Ayahuasca's unique recipe came together, but we know that it did, even if after so many centuries we still don't know what it quite is.

But we *do* know what Ayahuasca isn't.

It isn't toxic in normal quantities, normally prepared, and is in fact easy to digest beyond its pungently astringent taste. It's not addictive—potentially even being a cure for addiction–and even serious users might only do it a few times a year, nor is it some sort of deliriant that is upsetting your brain chemistry and risking turning you crazy.

At an experiential level, Ayahuasca isn't on the scale of normal drug "trips" being more bizarre, more engaging, more welcoming, and more manageable. It doesn't railroad you into uncontrollable hallucinations with the lingering threat of things going bad, because it seems not concerned with assaulting or entertaining you with extreme novelty that is ultimately confusing or pointless. By aligning with normal neurotransmitters, it doesn't introduce any foreign mechanism to your brain, instead heightening what is already there and metabolizing as usual.

But it is still a drug because despite being normal to metabolism, this particular combination and its effects don't happen without humans making it so. It just isn't acting in the usual drug way, but then neither is it acting in the way of any other thing, including its two ingredients individually, sort of making one plus one equal three or the whole being greater than the sum of the parts.

Culturally though, it fits right in with human use, as a species seemingly unable to live without taking some kind of drugs and availing itself to us by the simplest of means. As complex as the neurological and ontological aspects are, Ayahuasca's presence in our world could not be more seamless, as the result of intimate plant knowledge and the use of fire that the migrants to the Amazon arrived with.

Something else we also know Ayahuasca *isn't* is stupid. This is a drug where the last thing it does is dope you out or make you jittery and distracted, instead, it substantially heightens your cognitive functions so you are more attentive, patient, observant, intuitive, and all the other factors of intelligent behavior. Mood is stabilized with no real compulsion to extravagant or impulsive behavior, other than the awe and bemusement that comes with perceiving things so far outside normal experience. The whole weirdness and unexpectedness are certainly not lost, but it is neither orchestrated with orgasmic effusion nor panicky paranoia.

As odd as things seem, the hallucinations and rearranged perceptions make sense with a sort of self-contained logic, and intelligent investigation returns an intelligent response. There is no dumb giggly myopia like watching cartoons, instead, there is a seemingly bottomless series of levels of details for anything you wish to think about, question, or look into. Unlike the vacant staring into space found with things like cannabis, opioids, and tranquilizers, Ayahuasca finds all space and surfaces to be alive at any level, whether the breathing and pulsating surfaces at human-scale or the infinitely designed and interacting textures of anything upon microscopic observation.

You don't feel dumber after an Ayahuasca trip. You feel like you have traveled somewhere with high culture and picked up details and nuances that somehow bring dimension and meaning to life. You haven't been away, bombed out in some analgesic state, while the world goes on without you, rather you've been somewhere where data flows at a much higher rate.

Drugs, Psychedelics, and Tryptamines

The lexicon of Ayahuasca is rich and nuanced, covering multiple languages and cultural positions as it gets circulated by people with different perspectives.

We need to get over the negative connotations that go with the word "drug" and decouple it from the way it so often derails the conversation. In its way, *drug* is a useful word, differentiating itself from medicine, remedy, tincture, and food, maintaining its allusion to potency and ability to override normal bodily function. This is apt, and we shouldn't start using quasi-substitutes, but we need to be clear it is a term as generic as food, clothes, or work.

Drugs rightly have a certain reputation when the word is used collectively because it is often used to leverage an emotional response. Media adores the term for its capacity to create headlines and sensations, and subcultures use it to delineate themselves and exclude others. And some drugs do deserve their reputation as cultural definers or societal corrosives, as a visit to any substance rehabilitation facility will vividly show, but this association with the word can't be allowed to overshadow its other uses, any more than the junk sold with a drive-through should be allowed to define food.

Drugs, of course, have a history as long as humans themselves, probably evolving with us as primates and mammals as long as we have brains that react to chemicals. Goats go back to eating coffee, tobacco, and other stimulating plants, and cats famously eat catnip for no reason other than the effect. Drugs are part of our history–all of it–since long before we knew how they worked or felt the need to control them, with the history of drugs being the history of ourselves from making pain manageable to the politics of nations.

But not all drugs are psychedelics, not even most, and simply giving rise to hallucinations does not qualify a drug as psychedelic. "Psychedelic" itself means to externalize and manifest the psyche, effectively presenting the process of your mind so you can observe what it is doing. This means you are still you, anchored in this common world, and discounts drugs that are dissociatives or deliriants where the perception of self is changed. This means anesthetics, opioids, and tropanes are not psychedelic despite sometimes conjuring hallucinations, because these hallucinations are aberrations in the neurology rather than enhancements of it. Put another way, things like datura and opium cause visions because the brain and the perception of self are disrupted, whilst things like Ayahuasca, LSD, and MDMA cause visions because certain brain functions are enhanced.

Ayahuasca sits well outside the mundane terminology of the word "drug," even more so than the other tryptamines that can have a degree of recreational and exhilarating uses. Though Ayahuasca certainly has a pleasurable and enjoyable side, it sits perhaps closer to meditation than it does to the stereotype of a drug.

Tryptamines are the product of the metabolizing of tryptophan—a common amino acid found in all mammals, central to the maintenance of muscle and nerve tissue, and an "essential amino" meaning we have to consume it because our systems cannot make it. Drugs from the tryptamine group have certain qualities that relate them together, that distance them even from other psychedelics such as LSD and Mescaline, and this quality seems to be one of the logic of the experience. Where LSD's signature is an experience that is mostly voyeuristic and confronting, and mescaline is esoteric, evocative, and profound, the signature of the tryptamines is that they are engaging, linguistic, and clear.

The overall quality of the tryptamine experience is that *communication* is happening where information is being exchanged. Unlike LSD, which is like a show, and mescaline, which is a dance, tryptamines are a conversation and an intimate one at that.

Many people who take tryptamine psychedelics comment on things like the singing of the Ayahuasca, the chatter of the mushrooms, and the rapping, and raving of the DMT festival. These experiences seem to appeal to the language centers of consciousness and seem to have a two-way engagement where the user joins in. This quality is obvious enough that, unlike most other drugs, tryptamine psychedelics are heavily anthropomorphized, and referred to as things like guides, entities, and archetypes.

What this may mean neurologically is open to debate, probably being to do with activity in the brain centers for language. Ayahuasca and DMT in general seem to have an affinity with how things are conveyed and suggested by the fine motor processes of speaking and singing, which like much else of the experience might spill over to regular life.

What this means ontologically, is that there is a distinct feeling that this experience is to be understood and that the experience itself wants this and is engaging with its own logic. Just as a book exists to be read, music to be listened to, and a film to be seen, having all been created with that specific intent, tryptamine experiences have this quality that they are not merely to be observed, but contain information and reasons that are worth being conveyed.

Now, could this just be a phenomenon of consciousness, where the brain throws meaning and apparent logic into something actually random and inert? Yes, it could be, but for the scope of the phenomenon, that exceeds how this same thing usually happens. It is common for us to allocate sense and meaning to actually meaningless things, but in this case, what might be meaningless clearly communicates back, in a language we recognize, and in concert with our own thoughts.

Tryptamines communicate not in some obscure or coded way, but in actual words that you hear just like sound. DMT especially is loud, direct, and insistent, not unlike a drill sergeant, and often likened to a ringmaster. You are addressed personally, seemingly with the expectation to reply, with a kind of lexicon that includes questions, statements, and exclamations, and though the cadence of the dialogue is more song-like than tutorial, is fully comprehensible much like rap music or opera.

Now some kind of neural mechanism must be lighting up in the brain, for the simple reason that this dialogue is in whatever language you speak. Whatever it is, does not necessarily sound like, say, English, but is understood as such without translation, including very specific details. Spanish and Portuguese speakers get this in their languages, as do the speakers of the indigenous languages of the Amazon and presumably, their ancestors did too, and the chatter of psilocybin is heard in the languages of the places they are found including Japanese, Icelandic, and Czech.

Other drugs simply do not have this quality. They may have tones and buzzes or the soundtrack of delirium, but not even closely related psychedelics share the tryptamine family's insistence for talking.

Looked at as a product of nature in the same way that sunlight, vitamins, and aminos catalyze other metabolic processes, it is hard to dismiss this linguistic content as merely a meaningless product of a disrupted nervous system. What's more, this attribute is repeatable and expandable, where experience with the drugs increases communication, just as repeatedly traveling to a country enhances your ability to communicate there.

Ayahuasca vs Other Tryptamine Psychedelics

Are these things interchangeable in this conversation?

It is hard to quantify tryptamine psychedelics by experience, but for the sake of discussion let's say across these things there's maybe a sixty percent overlap where the nature of the experience can be said to have a "tryptamine quality," but beyond that things are starkly divergent.

The subject here is Ayahuasca. We will take it as a reference to the others, using its characteristics as the standard by which to differentiate the others. This in no way means that Ayahuasca is actually the standard, and in a book about any of the others, it would be explained in other ways.

DMT stands for DimethylTryptamine, specifically N, N-dimethyltryptamine, and is an analog of serotonin that can take its place in metabolism. Lots of people talk about it, but far fewer actually use it, and of those who try it not everyone does it again, let alone often. DMT, whilst a primary part of Ayahuasca, is a very different thing. Indeed, it could be said that straight DMT is unlike anything, anywhere, ever, and though the connection with Ayahuasca makes sense, it is not immediately obvious.

DMT comes as a yellowish crystalline material, looking somewhere between toenail clippings and flakes of orangeish snow. It is hard to get, though the emerging technology for vaping is providing a platform for its accessibility, and though it can be made covertly in laboratories, it is complicated so is usually extracted from organic matter.

Outside of Ayahuasca it is usually smoked, or more accurately freebased, where the crystals are vaporized at high temperatures into something that feels like smoking plastic. Fortunately, the required amount is only two or three moderate inhalations, after which there is just enough time to set down the pipe, lay back, and buckle up your seat belt.

What happens next makes even Ayahuasca seem mundane, though as bewildering as it is, it is predictable, repeatable, and ultimately manageable. A series of thresholds seems to need to be passed through, each exponentially escalating in beauty, detail, and novelty, starting with a sense of flying through sunlit fractals and coming to a head as the feeling of crash landing through the ceiling of a Faberge egg made of circuitry made of iridescent insects made of sea anemones. This happens over the span of about a minute and feels like it. There is no time distortion; it all happens with the urgency of fans rushing a Beatles concert, with everything in real-time as you sit there and watch.

Inside the Faberge egg, you realize the stage is being rushed, that you are the attraction, and are being swarmed with enthusiastic *things*. What these things are is hard to tell because they are fluid, changing their appearance as fast as you can keep up, but having a clear top and bottom, and usually eyes and mouths. They transition through shapes, textures, and forms like a mix of octopuses, puzzle cubes, origami flowers, and acrobats, whilst chattering in an obvious language that is unintelligible but somehow translated in your head.

This is where it gets weird.

Unlike hallucinations on other things where you just seem to be either a spectator or listener, the DMT things address you as familiarly as a teammate. They are encouraging you to watch them, and not to get distracted or scared—which, of course, is near-impossible for the human mind. It is some kind of show or demonstration, as they display their abilities to change shapes and produce more shapes, with an intense enthusiasm that borders on insistent. The show gets ever more complicated as the things they keep producing fill the space, with the distinct feeling of getting crowded that is accompanied by the feeling it's too much and some system has been over-saturated.

The colors start to go and there's a scramble to push these weird objects out of the way, so you can see more, but it all starts to deflate into itself like origami in reverse order. Things noticeably pack away, not just fade out or collapse into static, until it all is sucked through a point in space firmly fixed in normalcy. It's as if all this has been imposed over wherever you normally are, and when it leaves, it is drawn back through some peephole in space, waving and twittering as it goes.

It's been said that DMT isn't the strangest thing you have experienced, but is the strangest thing you *can* experience, with Terence McKenna famously saying that its real risk is death by astonishment. Where Ayahuasca is immersive, journeying, intimate, and engaging, DMT is overwhelming, instantaneous, startling, and inexplicable—but all in a good way.

Where Ayahuasca appears to explain things and seek resolutions, it seems the role of DMT is to astound you and to entertain. Unlike Ayahuasca which puts you into a part of the bigger process, DMT drops you into the center of the arena, puts you on a pedestal, then rolls out the orchestra and demands you conduct it. Quantum physics states there is no state of being an observer, and DMT goes a step further and makes the entire experience for your interest. The intelligence the experience is infused with comes right out to engage you, actually talking and launching at you intentionally to get you to engage.

Of course, engaging initially is difficult, because unlike with Ayahuasca where you are invited to take part, the DMT world surges at you, grabbing your attention, like the sort of attention you see in old footage of Beatles concerts.

Where Ayahuasca lasts long enough to go deep into the experience, DMT is over in minutes, a testimony to how rapidly these tryptamines are metabolized. There is a brief process of going from normalcy into the DMT space, then about five minutes of whatever it is before it's time to go and the whole thing just breaks down into crackling data and vanishes. Unlike Ayahuasca which leaves you tired but refreshed and contemplative, DMT leaves you feeling awe-struck, speechless, and amused. While Ayahuasca's message is clear and travels well back to this world, DMT's message is like trying to explain a smartphone to a bird.

Does DMT assist the Ayahuasca experience in any way? Well, it certainly gives it—and any experience—a yardstick for weirdness, which helps. Being the same stuff but expressed differently and some basic elements altered, it is valuable to know just how hyperdimensional things can go, and how if you can return from that OK then everything else will be fine.

Psilocybin is much closer to Ayahuasca at least regarding the general experience, but where Ayahuasca is intimately about you and your own journey through a world populated with character and interactions, psilocybin is more about the network of interconnection itself, the conduit between the living landscape and seemingly even beyond.

Psilocybin, like DMT and Ayahuasca, talks directly with you, but whilst Ayahuasca is guiding you on an epic voyage, psilocybin is like a dinner party with the forces of nature. The message of it seems to be very large and pervasive, where you fit in not as the actor of Ayahuasca or the director of DMT, but as the producer and cinematographer who is behind it all and who has bigger plans than the role of the individual.

Psilocybin chats, discusses, and explains, like one of the good teachers we all wish we had more of who has what we want to know but isn't just doling out answers for free. It seems to have a clear dialogue that has little of the craziness of something like LSD, being a much gentler and comprehensible thing that of all the tryptamines mentioned is also probably the most euphoric.

Psilocybin feels good, aside from the aspect of

purging that seems to depend on the mycological variety and is not nearly as defined as with Ayahuasca. There is a discernible tingle and buzz to psilocybin, where everything is felt to be alive with energy and intercommunication, including yourself. There is a palpable diffusion of boundaries, not a lostness of self, but it seems you can observe the exchanges between all meeting surfaces, much like the effervescence of a tablet dropped in water.

Psilocybin has about the same duration as Ayahuasca, as Alexander and Anne Shulgin said—it is what that day is going to be all about. Like Ayahuasca, it has a definite curve to the trip that has a peak phase, where the amount of information and connecting ideas going around can be more than the uninitiated thought was possible. Where Ayahuasca feels like it is taking place in a long stretch of history where things are ancient and evolved and have specific intents, psilocybin feels much more cosmic and fresh, like the cliche of a constant new day, measured in the lifetimes of galaxies down to the fluttering of a bug's wings.

Is psilocybin helpful for the Ayahuasca candidate? Yes, because it is a similar space, but no, because it doesn't go into all the healing stuff. No one is calling psilocybin medicine, despite its background of use for therapy and contemporary ideas about micro-dosing, probably because those who know psilocybin see it as about other things. Of course, hints of cosmic consciousness and the interplay of life will be beneficial, but not nearly as directly as with Ayahuasca, which seems to have that central to its role.

Ibogaine is the least common of this group, but probably the closest to Ayahuasca in its emphasis on healing and realigning mindsets over simply astounding you with raw experience or trips to the edges of consciousness. Ibogaine is relatively earthy, profound, and never trivial, and goes on for days to make it an ordeal in the Homerian sense, where time is a major player, across several phases.

Unlike Ayahuasca, it doesn't have a singular wave sign, having several, that are each very different and connected by phases of distinctly transitional experience. Where Ayahuasca is about its peak phase where things are most immersive, Ibogaine seems to be about navigating the transitions, a bit like a story where you choose the narrative based on your thoughts at certain junctures.

Ibogaine is not fun, and there is no recreational version, but as a transformative experience, it is well known and is beyond anything else. Ayahuasca cures and assists by realigning you with the directions of the natural world, but Ibogaine reduces you to your most basic—and then some—and rebuilds you better.

The dialogue of Ibogaine, as in the things you voice and the ideas you are presented with, seems to be your own voice, but from a primordial source that is stronger and more powerful. The visionary element is much more intensely cinematic, happening almost all behind closed eyes, and compared to Ayahuasca and psilocybin is far more personal and confronting.

There is no alien weirdness or festival stunts and twittering energy. Instead, Ibogaine paints in much broader strokes and pummels you with an intense feeling of confronting family or authority. This is the heavy lifting, and it is easy to see how it moves people on from things like heroin, as it is much more physical in every way than the other tryptamines and even LSD. The purging comes in cycles, stripping you to empty, and you are cycled through intense emotions but intelligently, feeling guided and with purpose. It is not hard to see how the indigenous uses of West Africa associated all this with ancestors and heroes of cosmology because this stuff knows it has a job to do and doesn't waste time on theatrics.

Does it help with Ayahuasca? If dealing with big issues is your intersection with tryptamines, then Ibogaine is the stuff, and if anything Ayahuasca might be preparation for it.

CHAPTER 1
Psychedelic Physiology

The brain can be looked at in numerous ways, as an organ, as a data organizer, and as a generator of realities. We have an idea of how complex it is, and a comprehension of how much information is flying around within it, but then we settle for only a single reality.

Everyday experience constantly confirms to us that reality is the intersection of information, both that which comes from outside our brains and that which the brain has already within it. It doesn't take much to see that both do not always seamlessly match up, with glitches and holes in the screen where we know things are not only as they present.

Drugs in general operate on this reality generation process, either reinforcing it or looking behind it depending on the way the drug's chemicals interact with the brain. Something like opioids powerfully reinforces a very low fi and simplistic experience, whilst Ayahuasca and similar drugs prop open the glitches and holes so we can experience reality expressed differently.

It's Already There

DMT, the primary active ingredient in Ayahuasca, is already present in the normal brain chemistry of primates, most higher mammals, and even most bizarrely in some species of fish. Why? No one knows, and quite a few have looked, putting forward all sorts of hypotheses ranging from being related to dreaming, quantum consciousness, death, and simply the formation of consensual experience and orientation of sensory experience. It also appears to have a protective action over neural tissue, but considering all this was only discovered in the mid-twentieth century and research has been retarded by legality for most of that and still is, it is still early days.

What we do know is that unlike almost any other drug the critical element has no need for introduction to the system and that whatever the psychedelic mechanism is it is about ratios rather than forced adaption or toxicity. DMT is so normal, and the precursors and metabolic pathways are so basic to human physiology, and indeed all higher mammals, that if you were to scan a person looking for some bizarre chemical gateway into other realities, it would be overlooked.

This mundaneness may well be what is behind DMT's potency, that rather than fiddling about with some exotic and peripheral process that covertly slides behind the reality generator that is the brain like picking a lock, changing the ratios of a primary neurotransmitter is more like jacking a house up onto a flatbed and driving away with the whole thing. This seems to be not about toying and tweaking with the latest updates, but about swapping out the interface entirely and yet using a means that is completely familiar and infers no shock to the body or damaging effect.

It is often commented how DMT and Ayahuasca have no real come-down or side effects, especially considering how profound and visceral the experience is. Where solid doses of LSD and Mescaline leave you in a state of exhaustion, and psilocybin feeling dreamy and jetlagged, DMT-based psychedelics seem to metabolize so seamlessly you are left normal if not mildly invigorated like having come off a rollercoaster.

Straight DMT itself returns you to normal metabolic function within half an hour, as long as it takes for the brain to assimilate the extra amount. Ayahuasca obviously takes longer as the DMT enters into the brain more slowly and the action of the beta-carbolines needs time to go through to the small intestine, then into the blood and carried to the brain. What is interesting is that even with this circuitous route, Ayahuasca still avoids a strong physical activity that leaves you frazzled and perturbed, further suggesting the action of the concoction in its entirety is entirely familiar to the body even when the MAOI process is engaged.

What Ayahuasca Does in the Brain

Our brains are startlingly welcoming to psychedelic tryptamines, immediately disposing of the myth that the psychedelic experience is caused by a state of confusion from the brain's various centers juggling around unknown chemicals until they find a way to be rid of them. Instead, the critical compounds that produce Ayahuasca's effects are effectively analogs of mundane compounds the brain uses all the time and seamlessly recognizes, making the experience caused by a shift in amount and ratio, rather than invasion by anything alien.

In the case of straight DMT, it arrives in the brain within a minute, measured in heartbeats as it goes from the lungs, just as fast as nitrous oxide at the dentist or the time it takes to register alarm bells by holding your breath. Delivered as Ayahuasca though, the DMT takes a scenic route via the small intestine and a series of major veins, then enters the brain gradually with an accumulative effect.

The all-important event with Ayahuasca, as with every psychedelic, is it is passing the blood-brain barrier. This is a layer of special cells that choose which compounds in the blood can pass to circulate through the brain. It's worth noting that only a tiny amount of introduced drugs can slip through this protective mechanism, making it one of the great frontiers of medical research.

Inside the brain, DMT has electrophysiologic, hormonal, and vascular actions. It has molecular affinities with the neurotransmitters serotonin and dopamine, connection to the same receptors apparently seamlessly by being structurally almost identical, More than one researcher has been amazed that something so similar that it can have uptake by the brain highly selective protective mechanisms, can have so profound an effect as to completely overwhelm perceived reality.

In the context of Ayahuasca, the DMT content is taken up by the brain at a slowed rate and combined with the beta-carboline tryptamines which are also similar to serotonin, to create an effect that combines mood and perceptual changes with the DMT's powerful hallucinogens. Alone, DMT is all-consuming, emotionally detached, and ultra-explicit, but in Ayahuasca the beta-carboline balance slows it down and makes it far more engaging.

The beta-carboline compounds have their own effects on the brain, being their own psychedelics, though much less profound when stood alone from DMT. The versions present in Ayahuasca—harmine, harmaline, and tetrahydroharmine—are responsible for potentiating the DMT by stimulating the central nervous system, stabilizing mood, and locking out serotonin so more DMT can be taken up thus extending its actions.

What Ayahuasca Does in the Body

Half of the Ayahuasca process is what happens in the digestive tract, which is effectively what sets it apart from DMT, which is usually smoked, so it enters the system via the lungs, making it much faster and more direct.

The Ayahuasca concoction on the other hand, is dissolved in water and drunk, entering the system via the digestive tract similar to alcohol or coffee, making it much slower and more metered. Like anything drunk, this process requires volume, which means a whole host of other compounds that carry the active ones to the nervous system. Where DMT is a pinch of crystals vaporized and the bulk of it passing straight to the brain across the large surface area of the lungs, Ayahuasca is the same active ingredient leisurely like a glass of wine, and this very process changes the entire experience.

This analogy with coffee and alcohol ends quickly because where they pass mostly effortlessly through the alimentary tract and into the blood, Ayahuasca requires a trick so the DMT within it escapes being broken down by the process of digestion.

This destruction of the DMT is a safety mechanism the body has evolved over time to safeguard against the entry of potentially toxic amino compounds, namely tyramine, an amino found in animal organs, chocolate, and things that have fermented. This is essential to our survival and is 99.9% of the time advantageous, except in this rare case where it can be done safely.

These potentially toxic aminos are destroyed by the action of Monoamine Oxidation, which needs to have the action suspended so the DMT can pass through the digestive tract. This of course has to be only temporarily, for as long as the DMT is present, and needs to happen with no toxic amino around, which is why many people will fast before an Ayahuasca session.

The Monoamine Oxidase process is turned off—or inhibited—by a group of compounds creatively called Monoamine Oxidase Inhibitors or MAOIs, which like a traffic light at an intersection shuts off one process so another can freely occur. These MAOIs have various types and are themselves psychoactive, with many people already being familiar with them for their use as antidepressants.

In the Ayahuasca concoction, it is the Bannisteriopsis Caapi vine that contributes to the MAOIs, in this case, a collection of beta-carbolines of the harmine group. Other versions of Ayahuasca not made from Amazonian plants use plants containing the same MAOIs found in other parts of the world, or in the case of purely synthetic "pharmahuasca" pharmaceutical MAOIs are used.

MAOIs have their own actions too, irrespective of potentiating DMT, increasing the flow of hormones like serotonin and dopamine that determine mood and likely affecting the Ayahuasca experience. Once making it through the gastrointestinal tract, the Ayahuasca is taken up by the bloodstream, and delivered to the brain in sustained duration over hours. The beta-carbolines are suspected of having their own psychedelic effects in higher doses, of the more peripheral and bodily type which might explain Ayahuasca's deeply immersive and visceral quality over the more visual quality of straight DMT.

Is It Real?

What your brain says is real, is real, so yes, what you experience on Ayahuasca is real. None of it is a trick, illusion, or contrived just for your entertainment, nor are the projections of a brain malfunctioning or in a profound state of confusion. Neurological research makes it clear the brain is doing nothing unordinary, other than increased activity in some areas caused by explainable mechanisms. Just as the brain is convinced that dreams and virtual reality are "real," so do with Ayahuasca visions and logic, only in this case there is no physical change such as the switching off of the body or the strapping on of technology.

Consider that right now you are sitting looking at letters on a page and constructing mental images and thoughts that exist somewhere between imagining them and perceiving them with a sort of mind's eye. The letters form words that you then turn into meaning and stories, with the ability for them to conjure your emotions and reactions, at a perceptual level, experiencing them as real. You are not asleep or daydreaming, your mind is alert and engaged. Greatly amplified, Ayahuasca is real in a similar way.

Whether it is what some people tell you is another matter, and where the contention lies, because every explanation is the front of an agenda and behind each is an ideology based on assumptions mixed with logic. Some people will tell you laughable things, based on half-baked pop "science" or corrupted religion, usually with the agenda of selling your something or somehow capitalizing on your attention. Others may have the agenda that it is no more than a neurological light show and an anomaly of chemistry, that it is as real as pornography and no more than a novelty.

It's too easy to simply reply to this with the counter-question "what does *real* mean?," a common dodging of what is a fundamental question and one at the root of the experience. The dodging of this question has been damaging to the entire research and discussion of psychedelics, trivializing it at least and criminalizing it at worst.

That the pillars of our cultures are so quick to dismiss this question of it being real, is itself an indicator of its realness, and brings weight to the matter. To some, the psychedelic experience is not real enough to be granted serious discussion, but is real enough to put people in jail or make them objects of fear mongering,

Ayahuasca is real in that it is not fake, and passes many of the other criteria for a "real" experience. These criteria include that it is repeatable; that other people separated by time, culture, location, and mindset have similar experiences; that changes made in the psychedelic state continue outside of it; that your physiology is not impaired or amplified during the experience; that you are not disengaged with this world during the experience; and that the things you encounter in the Ayahuasca world are not props or random misinterpretations of things from normal reality.

In other words, what you see, hear, perceive, and feel during the Ayahuasca experience is not like a movie that is constructed to appear a certain way outside of which actors, animators, and riggers make it appear realistic. Nor is it merely hallucination or tricks of the light where the mind is distracted or confused, and gives meaning like watching a screen full of static.

What separates tryptamine psychedelic states is that the things perceived can be interacted with and questioned, and looked into the details, all of which not only stand up to scrutiny but exceed it. Where the shadow on the wall turns out to be a tree branch and not a vampire, the creatures, objects, and light formations that appear within space on Ayahuasca don't disappear into logic when examined or recede when confronted.

When looked at closely, what you are watching is infinitely detailed, and like closing in on a bird's plumage or a flower's center, that detail continues, often exploding into even *more*. This hyper-detailedness is perhaps the most confirming that what is going on here is a type of reality because you don't need to go far for the sophistication of the details to exceed anything your casual mind can conjure. The mind doesn't just doze off blankly as detail and complexity lose fidelity, instead, increasing bizarreness and "aliveness" is perceived that hint at some other origin and reason for existing.

Things are not what they seem, they are more, and just because it is not what it appears to be doesn't mean it is not real. More than explanations are insufficient. In the same way that magic is real—that we know what we are seeing is not actually what is going on, no woman is being sawn in half—but that *something* is certainly happening and we are witnessing it, we just don't know what all the mechanisms are.

What Does It Mean?

Being outside consensual reality, what the Ayahuasca experience is and means is a Heisenbergian matter, where what anything is or means depends on what you infer upon it. More simply, just as beauty is in the eye of the beholder, so is every other value, including meaning, value, and simple definition.

Most modern western users of Ayahuasca try to work out what the experience is, and that effort takes up maybe half of the energy given to the experience, the rest going towards absorbing and seeking the benefits from it. Traditional users don't have this equation, having already a satisfactory explanation that fits their cultural model and explains everything about it.

Coming from outside these traditions makes explaining and accepting Ayahuasca very difficult because no modern western society makes room for such things. Elements of it are alluded to with explanations such as madness, hypnagogic states, linguistic perturbation, Jungian archetypes, and the dislocation of natural states such as dreaming and death, but it is a jumble of vague ideas that's more confusing than explanatory.

Traditional usage has none of this. The tribes and societies that have used Ayahuasca and parallel drugs for millennia have explanations that fit squarely into their worlds as unquestioningly as how to grow corn, hunt, and pass through puberty. There is a mix of what in our culture is called myth, legend, and folklore, with the hard day-to-day nature of living a tribal agrarian lifestyle. This matrix of explanations serves all the reasoning they need, and has done for many generations until we came along.

When first witnessed by westerners it was "explained" by the mindset of the era, which decided it was the product of the Christian devil, an explanation that satisfied outsiders for a few centuries after. The next waves of outsiders to try and explain it decided it was about things like telepathy, before replacing that with cold science that it was no more than the upsetting of chemical ratios in the brain. According to each model, it made sense, only to be rejected and replaced with new explanations as the means to quantify and investigate it evolved, with the last thirty years seeing something of a renaissance as other aspects of western society have developed around it.

What it all is, appears best explained as the reinterpretation of information used by the brain to structure reality, triggered by chemical changes. Normal processes for arranging reality based on fundamental things like time, identity, recognition, and the piecing together of sensory input are loosened so other experiences can come of them, but instead of being random, these altered perceptions happen along established formats related to our tribal history. This is why the experience of a modern urban westerner is so similar to that of an indigenous Amazonian because the ways that the wider bandwidth of information is expressed are following pathways in our neurology as connected to our "primitive" past as our taste receptors, names for colors, digestive enzymes, and hair colors.

This explanation obviously leaves a lot out, and will be as laughable in years to come as explaining it all as telepathy or voodoo, but takes into account that it is a bio-cultural event that is shared by both traditional and modern users. It lets go of the cultural relativism that tries to interpret it all solely from a modern pharmacological angle, and just as the Ayahuasceros explain, is as much about things like language and social perceptions as it is about neurotransmitters.

What it then *means*, takes on a different explanation, again sharing more with traditional use than the reductionist scientific explanation of quantifying it only by the brain's response. At a base level, it means there is an organized, self-referencing, and intelligent reality other than this one and you can experience it by changing the faculties of the brain to accept it. Unlike soporific, hyper-stimulated, or delirious states that some other chemicals induce by disrupting the brain, meaning they are just distortions of consensual reality—not forgetting that traditional peoples are well aware of those too—tryptamine psychedelic states are as "real" and have the same quality of meaning as everyday reality, only shared by fewer people and in a narrower context.

In traditional Ayahuasca-using societies, it *does* form part of consensual reality, but not the majority of it because it is too contained and specific. They hold that there are multiple realities, all as real as each other and relatively discrete, with valid meanings to each. This means to them that some things are better, or only, achieved in the Ayahuasca world, in most cases meaning things related to health, social dynamics, ancestry, sex, and future plans—things that in our modern world can also share other realities, such as those provided by alcohol, anesthetics, cyberspace, religion, and politics, which also shift values of common things but by familiarity we include in our single consensual reality.

This idea of compartmentalized realities for different functions means certain things are done in certain ones that might be inappropriate in others, or simply less effective. Just as you can't express certain thoughts in things like confessionals or online platforms, so Ayahuasca allows a world where you can express things about healing, people, and life plans.

Looked at this way, the meaning is straightforward—some realities are better than others for getting certain things done, and rather than bending one to accommodate things that may not fit it such as mental states like PTSD, depression, and existential confusion, you go to an appropriate one better suited to the task. This is not that unusual when you consider how many people need the drunken state to socialize, the hum of tranquilizers to relax, or the effects of opioids to cope with a spectrum of pain. Whilst those realities are more corruptions of this consensual one where the body is leveraged for consensual effect, the Ayahuasca reality makes almost no bodily changes, thus allowing things like emotions and quantitative faculties to stay intact in order to direct the experience.

It means something that normal language only extends to the fringes of the Ayahuasca experience. Then the further you go into the feelings, visual hallucinations, and sense of state, the more words and their use of them drop away. This same thing happens in all languages, not just English and including the indigenous language of the traditional users, and is a mechanism of psychedelics. It is clearly not like the *inability* to speak properly as found with things like alcohol or barbiturates, or even the hyperactive chatter of stimulants ranging from coffee to cocaine, instead, it is the peeling off of *language* as a means of defining and organizing an experience, where the faculties we have developed growing up find their limits. Just as a ten-year-old won't have the vocabulary or references to understand Mandelbrot fractals no matter how they are explained even though they are clearly observed, the mature and literate mind hasn't the references and the words don't exist to do more than superficially describe the full-blown Ayahuasca experience.

This again has a simple meaning—that far more exists than the brain is able to inform us consensually about. Beyond what our perception displays is not a fuzzy, mish-mash of a world without meaning, but rather a highly organized and alive one that happily goes on with or without our interaction. This world cannot be consensually explained because the very faculties for doing so don't apply there any more than a snorkel applies to skydiving, but this world is accessible nevertheless and even navigable.

CHAPTER 2
Entheogenic Medicine

First and foremost, Ayahuasca is about healing. Where DMT is concerned with the mechanisms of reality and psilocybin is about the breadth of consciousness, Ayahuasca concerns itself with solving problems between humans and their environment.

Ayahuasca is seen by many as something that fixes problems, including some of the indigenous people who use it as well as many urbanites a world away. This is an over-simplification and by far only a small part of where Ayahuasca can go, and when it is used for healing, it's by very different methods than what the standard concept of medicine encompasses.

Medicine. Sort of.

Ayahuasca has a long history of therapeutic use, so in a general sense that earns it the qualification as a medicine. Traditional use sometimes associates it with healing disease, though through mechanisms not really supported by modern medical theory, other than a psychosomatic element that has long been well known.

There is a problem with calling something a medicine that implies a compound or drug that cures, either fixing the physiological problem or alleviating the symptoms—neither of which Ayahuasca does. Maybe there is a process by which it rectifies things like serotonin and dopamine function in the brain to help fix mood disorders, but as yet successes with things like depression, addiction, and trauma are associated with Ayahuasca's capacity to change behavior.

Labeling something a medicine simply because it is taken as a drug, is a shallow and superficial way of approaching treatment. Whilst Ayahuasca may well initiate improvement with some conditions, it is the actions and reactions of the user that are doing the healing. Not unlike going to counseling or psychotherapy, it is the space, the process, and the interaction with a professional that both initiate and direct any progress and in the case of Ayahuasca the things that do this are the shaman and the perceived character of the drug.

As the drug itself, in straight chemical form, Ayahuasca won't probably heal anything. You have to take the trip and all that goes with it, like the purging and hallucinating, to set up the conditions for any healing to happen. In this light, it barely ranks as a medicine at all, instead being a therapy closer to massage or fasting. The drug element does, though, give it a definite mechanism that is much more tangible and effective than therapies that are more subjective.

Labeling it as a medicine raises other problems that come from the perspective of modern medicine, and that don't really concur with Ayahuasca's traditional use. Much of these issues are based on the expectations of medicine as we think of it, and the role medicine has in curing disease.

Modern societies see medicine as something that is prescribed by professionals and has a specific action. This idea is neat and clean and fits into an industrial and commercial society, and is a pillar around which our entire social systems revolve. But Ayahuasca doesn't work this way, and efforts to hammer it into this format can make for skewed ideas and expectations about its use.

Ayahuasca does not follow the doctor-patient relationship model that modern medicine does, which changes things like personalization, accountability, and dosage. The role of the shaman or guide in an Ayahuasca experience would be the roles of about five people in the medical world, including pharmacist, doctor, therapist, and psychiatrist.

Often the person who makes the Ayahuasca concoction is also leading the session and takes an intimate level of involvement every step of the way. This is unheard of in medicine where it is even rare for a doctor to be present when medicine is taken, and stretches the term medicine fundamentally, it is based on the patient's autonomy.

Medicine is made, packaged, dosed out, and prescribed explicitly so the consumer can take it themselves. Ayahuasca is not.

Ayahuasca is usually taken with the shaman overseeing the timing and amount, and adjusting to suit the unique settings and person. Furthermore, the shaman themselves will usually have taken some too, to both understand the characteristics of the brew and to be in the same timeline and mindset as everyone else.

This relationship makes the entire thing unique and blurs objectivity, and removes the Ayahuasca concoction from being an intermediary in the healing or therapeutic process. In fact, it is better said that it is the shaman that does the healing, and that the drug merely sets the stage for them to do their work. This means that any expectation of simply taking the drug will have the effect, such as with actual medicine, and that a certain dose in a certain time is as black and white as taking tablets from a blister pack.

The inference then is that the idea of self-medication is also scuttled, which is a common case with many illegal, traditional, or misused drugs. Of course, Ayahuasca can be taken alone, and the effects will be present, but the therapeutic element will be radically different because of the absence of the shaman and setting. Unlike cannabis, alcohol, opioids, and a whole array of pharmaceuticals that are common as coping agents for undiagnosed or mistreated problems, Ayahuasca without the shamanic setting doesn't have the immediacy or casualness to solve or alleviate personal problems and goes off into other things perhaps closer to what is found with LSD or MDMA, namely psychedelic experiences that are more exploration than healing.

Lumping Ayahuasca in with "alternative medicines" is a fundamental mistake that says more about popular media than anything to do with the drug. Ayahuasca fills no alternative space and has no action that would be described as medicine, instead when used for the sake of healing, it addresses problems along its own course.

Simply because something can heal does not make it medicine, including cases much more prosaic than tryptamines such as massage and sleep. To try and view Ayahuasca as only a way of being cured makes it complex and corrupted from the start, setting up problematic expectations and demands that may not be met to someone's detriment.

A signature of much alternative medicine is that it opposes conventional medicine on all sorts of grounds from the conspiratorial to the commercial, and sometimes not without argument, at least theoretically.

Ayahuasca and tryptamine therapy in general usually don't do this, instead being something that overlaps with conventional medicine because of its body of research.

Ayahuasca is so clearly related to accepted pharmacological, botanical, and physiological theory it has little need to contest what modern medicine upholds, and even less the need to compete as an industry. Research, though still in its infancy, clearly shows what psychedelic tryptamines do, either confirming what is suspected or extrapolating on what is known.

There are no conspiracies around psychedelic tryptamines so they don't really compete, and the therapeutic uses are for things that society, in general, wants to see addressed. Where once in the mid-twentieth century claims and research around things like LSD were hazy, dishonest, and even at times sinister, the new era of more sophisticated and reliable psychedelics has largely been with the interest of science, not the suspicion.

Depression

Ayahuasca's potential to heal lies in its capacity to shift perspectives, to step away from mindsets and behaviors that can lock ways of thinking and act into place. This is both a chemical and behavioral equation, as anyone who has sought treatment for depression will know, with Ayahuasca having a profound effect on both.

Tryptamines are fundamentally linked to brain function, including the way hormones affect moods by the amount present in parts of the brain. Ayahuasca is well known for the effects it has on mood, even under the most profound of psychedelic states that would trigger stress and anxiety in something like LSD, keeping an even keel and buoyant state that allows for prolonged periods of contemplation.

Perhaps the biggest indicator of Ayahusaca's ability to regulate mood and mental state orientation is during the come-down, a phase notorious with other psychedelics for being uncomfortable, distracting, depressive, and lost, but Ayahuasca can be revitalizing and invigorating.

Like with all brain functions, Ayahuasca seems to act directly on the pathways and neurotransmitter levels, working with the brain rather than against it as so many other drugs do. Where things like serotonin relate to depression when the production and uptake are low, Ayahuasca appears to make up the difference and ratio.

Half of Ayahusaca's potential is in its capacity to recompose behavior—and any behavior regardless of its relation to depression or not. People without such issues find they are able to reassess and realign aspects of their lives, so it makes sense that behavior around depression can be addressed too.

Chemically, Ayahuasca is very close to prescribed antidepressants, something that attracts many who seek it as a way to both treat their condition and get off the medications. Recognizing the same chemical compounds as they see on the packet for their medication provides a bridge of familiarity they are not going too far into bizarre concoctions, and provides some of a roadmap for what to expect. This alone is a factor in addressing depression, the continuity of chemicals, and the building of positive patterns in a worldview, presenting an alternative that is also fundamentally related.

Ayahuasca appears to be less linked to being a trigger for depression than Cannabis, another plant drug that is gradually losing its bad reputation and becoming slowly decriminalized in much of the world. Cannabis is associated not just with having some risks for triggering depression but more so with being a form of self-medication chosen by people who already suffer from it, with inconsistent results when it comes to helping.

Ayahuasca, comparatively, shows a high significance for alleviating depression, both at a neurological level where it contains the compounds that pharmaceutical antidepressants use and at a behavioral level for altering thought sequences. Where

Cannabis has a significant risk of instilling a depressive lifestyle due to misuse and over-identification, Ayahuasca, by its nature as being more exotic, has a lower chance for habituation and therefore the extended effects of its use past the actual experience.

Addiction

To many, the idea of taking a drug to break an addiction to drugs seems absurd, but the concept is fundamentally sound of using one kind of chemical process to overcome another, and psychedelics themselves have a long history of being used to rectify various forms of addiction. Psilocybin has been used to treat alcoholism and indeed that was part of its early research, and Ibogaine—the powerful tryptamine that originates among tribal use in Central Africa—has been extensively shown to treat addictions to opioids and even nicotine. Addiction itself needs to be broken down into its various aspects, and doing so starts to clarify the way in which tryptamines can have an effect.

The early days of psychedelic research were very focused on their capacity to counter addiction, with Timothy Leary famously saying that "good drugs, displace bad drugs." This notion was quickly dismissed with the overwhelming though erroneous one that good drugs *lead* to bad drugs, and investigation into the potential was soon diverted or dismissed.

Tryptamines like Ayahuasca themselves are not

addictive, yet act on the brain centers that modulate addictive responses and behavior. Addiction itself is made up of multiple facets including chemical dependence, habitual behavior, stress avoidance, identity distortion, and secondary substance interaction—all of which Ayahuasca is shown to have an impact on independently.

The neural pathways of addiction, whatever the drug, are directly acted by Ayahuasca as they are by other endogenous transmitters. Even Dopamine pathways, which are particularly prone to addictive cycles, are modulated by Ayahuasca rather than disrupted.

What appears to be happening is that Ayahuasca aligns with the nerve tissue itself, rather than the drugs running through it and that damage or disruption to the neural connections is corrected to function more normally, suspending the effects that addictive drugs have which the body gets caught up in. Extensive studies show that people using Ayahuasca for addiction have a high success rate for reducing the severity of addiction, rehabilitation from addiction, and remaining unaddicted for long-term periods after.

Post-Traumatic Stress Disorder

Perhaps more than anything, Ayahuasca has been researched and advocated for its benefits to people suffering Post Traumatic Stress Disorder, which is a series of interrelated conditions in reaction to a single or series of traumatic events. Maybe a matter of Ayahuasca's rise in exposure at the same time as many western nations entered into the traumatic events of the protracted war on terrorism that generated a large number of sufferers, it has become synonymous with this too many.

From an Ayahuasca perspective, it walks the line between medicine and therapy, where the drug concoction itself is often the agent of focus, overshadowing the role of the larger psychedelic and shamanic elements. As described earlier, this has run the risk of Ayahuasca being seen as a wonder pharmaceutical, especially in a media wanting to exploit it as part of an agenda.

The actual mechanisms of Ayahuasca for this purpose are split into two; the pharmacological effects of the drug on the brain, and the psychedelic effects of the trip on mindset and behavior.

PTSD is a complex combination of disorders across a range of factors affecting behavior and psychology. At its core, the condition has an endocrine mechanism, where hormones in the brain are triggered out of context to events, and an anatomical element with the brain's glands suffering the effects of over-stimulation.

Beyond the brain, PTSD sets up behavioral

problems that are either uncontrollable or hyper-reflexive, including things like flashbacks, panic attacks, hyper-vigilance, avoidance sequences. PTSD is caused by a profound event that dislocates a person's mental strategies, reactions, and perspective. It can have an immediate or delayed onset ranging from minutes to years, and the condition itself can be temporary, long-term, or permanent. Some cases go unreported or unrecognized or can be hidden within or confused with other disorders.

Historically, PTSD has a checkered past, of misdiagnosis, denial, poorly informed and executed treatments, and a significant amount of stigmatization that includes stereotypes, self-medication, ignorance, and exploitation. In many ways, it was not until the turn of the millennium that PTSD became clearly accepted and defined, by either the medical and therapeutic communities or the insurance, government, and social ones that are involved in the costs.

Psychedelics have an extensive history associated with PTSD, from early theories and experiments with psilocybin to decades of uncontrolled self-medicating, then the emergence of serious discussion and research that had Ayahuasca at the center. Long claimed by traditional users for this kind of thing, Ayahuasca has an obvious relation to trauma disorders at both a chemical and therapeutic level.

In the brain, Ayahuasca affects precisely the same neurotransmitters that, in the case of PTSD, can be low compared to the amounts found in non-traumatized people. The beta-carbolines and DMT precursors appear to modulate or normalize the secretions of serotonin and dopamine, evening out levels that are low and adjusting ratios so they are in equilibrium.

Behaviorally, the DMT aspect appears to loosen the user attachments to strict rules for reality, something normal users expect and enjoy, but in the case of trauma, sufferers provide a valuable break from the feedback loops they are stuck with. The presence of hallucinations heightened perception, and altered moods for *understood and rational* reasons let them observe their mindset and reactions with some objectivity and create some distance from their effects.

Neurogenesis and Neuroplasticity

Of profound interest in Ayahuasca is its apparent ability to promote the creation and structuring of nerves in the brain, called neurogenesis and neuroplasticity respectively. Where many drugs limit, hardwire, and calcify—if not damage—nerve tissue, the fact that psychedelics including Ayahuasca do the opposite is pretty special stuff, what's more, that Ayahuasca may do both.

Were a holy grail to exist, it surely is the ability to regrow and rebuild neural pathways to inhibit things like aging, plateaued learning, and neurodegenerative disease. And whilst no one is seriously implicating Ayahuasca in things like immortality and super-intelligence, these things are potential answers to huge issues that face all humanity.

Neurogenesis is the generation of new nerve cells in the brain, more specifically the neurons, which are the cells that build nerve systems. The creation of new brain nerve cells in humans is something overwhelmingly done in gestation, and slows off by about the third trimester, then for the rest of our lives is limited to only a few parts of the brain associated primarily with memory and moods.

Neuroplasticity is the formation of nerve pathways that form new connections that carry memory, allow learning, and rebuild ones that have deteriorated. This happens either by producing new nerve cells from neurogenesis, or the reorganization of existing ones. In the case of Ayahuasca, early research shows that the level of DMT it includes can induce neuron production, but that larger doses like what's found with straight DMT don't have this effect or even reverse it.

Interestingly, nearly all known chemicals that have this neuroplastic action, known as *psychoplastogens*, are either psychedelic or hallucinogenic, including not only serotonergic tryptamines like Ayahuasca, but psychedelic and hallucinogenic drugs from right across the spectrum including Ketamine, Scopolamine, and

MDMA which very different orders of drugs altogether. Of these, Ayahuasca is arguably the lowest risk due to having the least impact on the body, as already described by the affinity it has with the normal chemistry of the brain.

Psychedelics have long been linked to this process by assumption as a way to remap brain circuitry and form new connections. Phenomena such as synesthesia, where sensory information is crossed so things like sound appear and a visual image and texture have flavors, have been suggested as evidence for this cortical remapping, though the effects are usually only temporary.

These abilities to "rewire" the brains pathways, though barely researched, have their origins in the history of psychedelics which include dubious ideas about things like brainwashing, gay conversion therapy, and lowering the inhibitions of soldiers as much as they do about treating people for suicidal behavior, increased learning capacity, treating the effects of aging, and researching brain function,

It must be stressed that these findings are in the very early days and mostly speculation, though speculation that is informed. The illegal nature of things like DMT and Ayahuasca slows down research at every level, including the uptake of interest by communities. This is a frontier of Ayahuasca, among the many that present, and though it may not be a short-term cure for things like Alzheimer, it is one where the average user can be involved, with modern society being the first to see the overlap of advanced longevity and widespread psychedelic tryptamine use.

CHAPTER 3
Shamanism

Shamanism is based on the idea that the world of common experience is only one world that exists, and that accessing these other worlds can be a way to fix or better understand things that are not understood here. Often portrayed as mystical and bizarre, in practice, shamanism can be more mundane and prosaic, usually not having the concepts around divinity and sacredness that more modern religions make central as a way to separate what they believe to be special and what's not.

Shamanism as a defined thing is usually centered on it having a shaman, though there are other aspects of what is a diverse array of practices that may better define it. Unlike most established religions that revolve around special central figures like deities, gurus, priests, and the enlightened, the shamans of shamanism are usually not considered special.

Shamanism is the core belief system of humanity, where it first became organized as a way to explain the world. It arose when we still had an integral role within the natural world, pre-agriculture, so fixated on the things we shared our world with, like animals, plants, and natural phenomena. These things were seen to have independent thought as we do, so assumed to also have inner worlds like ours where they dreamed and went when they died. These were seen as channels where humans could connect with them on a plane less individuated as separate species or events, with methods including drug use as a way to enter it.

Belief Before Religion

Shamanism predates all other religions, possibly to be considered the proto-ideology from which what has come since is derived. It is the belief that there are more worlds than the one we communally experience, that they intersect and interact with each other and that some people and places or objects are intermediaries between them. In some societies, shamans are specially selected and extensively trained and hold a special place in society. In others, anyone can take on the role when the conditions are present.

Shamanism was humanity's first organized system of philosophy and spirituality, and the start of the hierarchy paradigm that eventually became both the religions and sciences of today. This was the first way our ancestors made a separate class and role for beliefs, in an effort to explain and interact with things we saw no utilitarian reason for.

The first indications of shamanism go back around 50,000 years using the definition of shamans as indications of a developed sense of religion. This means that they existed before this as well, during the long process of evolution of human culture and thought. This definition is centered on shamans having rituals and implements as found by archeologists, showing a distinct job in a society that required things like organization around making objects and ideas that were not only for basic survival. Early evidence also finds shamans buried as such, with the accouterments of their role such as puppets and animal bones, showing that it was a specific cultural position that others treated as special enough to need ritualized burial.

Though usually associated with places like the Amazon, Siberia, Africa, and Australia, shamanism is present in all corners of the world including China and Japan, all across Europe, and North America. Chinese writing, the oldest continuously used writing method there is, had its origins in shamanism as a way to divine the patterns in cracked tortoise shells.

Animals seem to have been central to all strains of shamanism, whether psychedelics were used or not, often seen as relatives of ours that filled other niches, and had effects on the world different from ours. Where psychedelic shamanism seems to differ sometimes is in the way that with some animals we could assume or merge with their identity, probably brought on by the perceptual changes of the psychedelic state which very closely feel like flying, changing size, and being underground.

A common visual experience with Ayahuasca and DMT is seeing a vista of high above a detailed landscape of rivers, mountains, coral reefs, and sandbars, that can instantly shift to the same visual imagery that is actually an intense close-up of the veins of leaves, patterns of moss, and structures of things like feathers and insect wings. These are very common tryptamine visuals, to the point of being one of Ayahuasca's signatures, and make the idea of assuming an animal's consciousness easy to entertain.

Entheogenic drugs appear to have been only relevant to a selection of shamanic activities, obviously being limited to the places where they could be found. It is a mistake to equate them specifically with shamanism because there are other things far more common to shamanism around the world such as drumming, painting, trance states, and the arrangement of oracle implements.

Our ancestors may well have eaten hallucinogenic plants long before they were formed as part of any organized belief system, as part of a foraging lifestyle that we evolved as we came out of the oceans. Just as mammals and primates would have learned through trial and error of what could be eaten or not, things that resulted in psychedelic states would have been just part of life.

Pranksters, Charlatans, and Ayahuasceros

Peruvian and Amazonian shamans are called Ayahuascueros, and they come from a dedicated life where the matter of Ayahuasca is as much a job and a career as being a doctor, pilot, or chef. This is not a casual role, and though good and bad versions exist, they are as renowned or despised for their work as anyone with any other trade.

Western popular culture is very good at generating self-anointed "gurus" who go from new-age trend to trend, playing the latest thing that will get them at the center of a group of adoring but naive acolytes. The worst are serious cult leaders with disturbing intentions that prey on the seeking, but most are no more than superficial characters opportunists on the gullibility of others for a shallow ego trip.

Ayahuasca is no stranger to this matter, harking back to the LSD gurus of the 1960s, the primal scream leaders of the '70s, the tantric yoga gurus of the '80s, and countless other easy marks since then, with drug-centered groups being a particularly easy touch because they combined supplier with a leader.

Authentic shamans exist, and some cultures like

those of the Amazonian people and Southern African tribes, the animists of Indonesia, the peoples of Australia and North America that survived colonization, and the Altaic and Tuvan people of Mongolia and Siberia, still have them as integral societal members. These people fulfill a role within modern society that is an overlap of medical, spiritual, and practical and is often surprisingly prosaic with them having other 'day" jobs like being mechanics, construction workers, and government employees.

For many, being a shaman is a social role, with a set of skills and rites they must learn and use, and carries no more adulation than being a dentist or policeman, and in many cases is stigmatized as being an outsider or frightening. Needless to say, this is different to the modern urban idea of the shaman, which is highly fantasized and speculative and frequently exploited by new-age publishing. This dreamt-up version is mostly an amalgam of orientalism and urban mythology, not helped by films and television that use shamans as plot mechanisms.

The popular press has had a long-standing love of the shaman character, as a way to portray the otherness or "primitive" traits of people considered exotic or relics of the past. Organizations like National Geographic for decades had shamans as a handy trope for showing what it portrayed as bizarre and sensational cultural sideshows, very often to illustrate the backdrop of a story about brave scientists and explorers who encountered them.

These portrayals were products of their time, misguided in their intentions but usually with the idea of showing the diversity of the world. Far more condemnable is the contemporary adoption of self-appointed gurus, who continue many of these shallow or erroneous memes of the past to coerce people and profit from them. These days the new age press is full of people who deck themselves out and follow "their calling" as shamans. Rarely does it seem with the integrity of the real thing or the accountability to go with it.

The divide between the real thing and out-right con artists is not as black and white as it seems, and the characters that act as guides and wingmen for the Ayahuasca experience don't always fall into easy stereotypes.

The trickster or prankster should not be assumed to be also a huckster or con artist, and actually forms a fundamental part of many shaman traditions. Even established psychedelic shamans often have humorous and complex characters, and use tricks and illusions of the mind to display its fragility and glitchiness as a projector of reality.

The well-known fictional character of Carlos Castenada's books, Don Juan, provides a near-archetype of the trickster, taking the act of pranksterism way out to demonstrate the nature of perception and reality. Probably an amalgamation of several people Castenada knew of, his identity or authenticity is irrelevant but his lessons are real.

Perceived reality is not always to be taken too seriously because the mechanisms by which reality is experienced don't always follow a logic that is predictably clear. Just as comedy functions on the mechanisms of incongruity, surprise, juxtaposition, alternate meanings, confrontation, and being misled, so too does the forming of reality where few certainties exist.

Humor may well be the shaman's real skill, because of its way to cut through every other mood and assumption. Humor exists, we all experience it as so and even share a lot of it, forming a consensual mechanism that lets us unpick consensual perception. The very best magicians know this, and employ humor as a way to shape and direct perception, knowing full well that the mind pleased by what it sees also takes pleasure in believing the illusion. Once the illusion is accepted, it can be manipulated and extrapolated, without having to account for representing "cold hard reality," something with a huge overlap with the psychedelic experience.

This tricksterism is as different from charlatanism as a magic show is from fraud, with tricksterism highlighting the mechanisms of perception whilst fraudulence deceives you. The goal of a trickster is to heighten your reality and show you behind the curtain. The goal of the charlatan is usually your money, in a ratio far more than their act is worth.

Charlatans and posturing ego-trippers abound, and Ayahuasca has its fair share of both surrounding it as psychedelics of all sorts have long attracted people wanting to exploit their capacity for personal change. The charlatan will claim to provide all the answers for the things you are willing to pay for and sees you not as somebody exploring, but as someone with money to spend.

Of course, authentic shamans need to make a living and be given value for what they do, but the transaction is for their work, not for the promise of some psychedelic goal. The charlatan won't operate this way and will define their price by the work that you yourself will be doing, such as resolving personal matters, exploring consciousness, and developing your perception. Like mountain guides, the real ones will get you to climb better and see into your abilities, while the phonies will simply drag you up a mountain, and back down in time for dinner. The difference may not always be discernable at the time, but later becomes clear, because one has been learning to climb whilst the other has been learning to be led.

Just like a good climbing guide, any real shaman

will tell you the process is to become independently better, and they will demonstrate it directly by letting you see what you can do. The real shaman will direct you to have your own experience, push you if you won't, and impose only as much of their own experience as is needed to demonstrate and keep things on track.

The real Ayahuascero is part flight controller, part wingman, part navigator, but never the pilot because that role is yours. Far from the led meditations and guided experiences the new age community trades on, Ayahuasceros fill the role of the remover of obstacles.

These obstacles most often are the pillars of perception that benefit from the playbook of tricks, rites, songs, and antics of the Ayahuascero to loosen up and work around. Starting with the concoction, they will begin constructing the journey, forming a plan for the methods and directions to take, with the finest Ayahuasceros drawing from a vast tool kit of ways to release the experience and show you through it. Like a master theatrical director, they know all the mechanisms backstage, as well as how it presents to the audience and all the lines and actions of the cast. Being live, every time different and unique events always arise, and their work is to keep the show unfolding so everyone can draw meaning and intimacy from it.

This is not the art of illusion, which is what the charlatans are playing at, but the craft of shaping the illusion by using the faculties of perception. How real and meaningful the experience can be is what the Ayahuascero abilities enhance, getting you far beyond a "drug trip" and into the realities normal consciousness must be prepared for.

The Mystery of the Mixture

We have all heard about the tropical forests of South America—loosely termed "the Amazon"—with the various descriptors of its size, diversity, and relation to all life on the planet, but it's not always clear to everyone just what this place means.

At a rough measurement, the Amazon rainforest is around 7 million square kilometers, which makes it almost twice the size of India, the same as the contiguous US, three-quarters the size of Australia, or nearly thirty times the size of Great Britain. Accounting for more than half of all tropical forests on the planet, the Amazon has a third of all species known of *anything* outside the oceans, so the fact that it would also produce plants with compounds that take us far into our nervous systems should not be alarming. This same ecosystem gives rise to species like the electric eel,

How the combination of the various plants that make Ayahuasca active and safe was arrived at has been considered both a mystery and an astounding act of chance by many who consider such things. We know that humans entered the Amazonian environment as fully fledged, intelligent humans with the same brains we have today, but a leftover of monotheistic creationism is that our species entered the world unknowing and ignorant and had to find out everything new through trial and error and revelation. This is absurd.

By the time humans arrived in the Amazon they had migrated for tens of millennia from Africa, indeed the farthest it is possible to migrate, and been exposed to almost all types of ecosystems along the way. Humans arrived in the Amazon with perhaps the greatest amount of stored knowledge in pre-literate history, which gave them an unprecedented perspective when it came to the interactions and values of plants in such a huge area of diversity.

Approximately 15,000 years or 750 generations ago, on top of 45,000 years before that, which already began in a region known to have psychedelic plants from the start. These modern humans, every bit as cognitive as we are as you read this, would have known plants that have had these effects since before they left Africa. It can be considered logical that having these things in our diet is no less unusual than any other fruits, seeds, or animals we eat, predating our species from earlier versions.

Whether or not psychedelics in part drove things like migration and the evolution of culture as proposed by thinkers and explorers like Terence McKenna is one thing and based on a lot of assumptions, but to think that a species that could navigate and survive crossing the planet during an ice age could concoct something like Ayahuasca is not. The fact exists that they did.

By the time of arrival they had passed through central America, an area already rich in psychoactive plants, and before that what was the north American and Siberian tundra and birch forest with their well-known fungi, and even before that with the psychoactive plants of Asia and the fertile crescent. Whilst they may have been in a primitive state of technology, these people were by no means in a primitive state of intelligence, with a combined cultural knowledge of plants as food and psychoactives surpassing anything of today.

Just as cultures intimately pick up on the nuances of taste, smell, reaction, and effect, so too the inhabitants of the Amazon basin would have discerned how different plants acted when consumed, coming to know each species before they would have combined them. It is less likely to assume they merely stumbled across the Ayahuasca admixture than they had ideas about what it would do and pursued it intentionally.

The idea that the overwhelming diversity of the Amazon raises the chances of finding two plants that work together is a false logic, based on the assumption that people were not seeking for this effect.

CHAPTER 4
Taking Ayahuasca

For many, the entheogenic element is integral to the experience and cannot be removed for fear of losing the language and context upon which the Ayahuasca makes sense, but for others, they find that it extends beyond cultural definitions and that there may be no quintessential Ayahuasca culture.

The standard procedure for taking Ayahuasca is in a group, usually with someone who is familiar with it and acts as an overseer, in a setting that is relaxed and secure for the duration of the event. People spend time relaxing and drinking the brewed concoction until they have drunk what is considered enough, then relax as the effects come on and talk and interact over the hours of the experience.

Like most other psychedelics, the effects increase and become immersive, peak for a time, then subside gradually and tail off. This curve to the experience is well-known, reliable, and expectable and people go through it roughly at the same pace, which forms a sense of unity and shared insights because they are together as things occur.

Unlike the hysterical perception of psychedelics by demonizers, Ayahuasca and indeed all tryptamines don't get "crazy,: intense, or "freaky," and things stay fairly relaxed and would be seen as boring or lazy to the non-imbibing observer. Ayahuasca generates a talkative and contemplative mood but not one that is agitated or effuse, and the feeling of connectedness is tangible which lays things open for engaging and listening, being very different to things like alcohol, stimulants, or cannabis.

Ayahuasca doesn't feel trivial because perception is so different and the mindset so profound, with a distinct sense that you are seeing more into things that are otherwise not apparent. There is a present but not overwhelming euphoria that is more a product of the experience than a cause of it, where the depth and quality of your thoughts are of much higher fidelity than normal and the visual quality is aesthetically very impressive.

There are no kaleidoscopes, at least not in the starburst, cliched "acid" way that movies portray it, but with eyes closed there are vistas and moving forms that can be heart-rendering beautiful, that continue over to eyes-opened as peripheral phenomena and occasionally manifest as part of objects such as surfaces, sound, and movement.

The most invasive thing to occur is the action of vomiting or releasing the bowels, which comes on rapidly but not suddenly and is easily purged, and has no association with illness or poisoning, being more like having drunk too much fruit juice or eaten too much oil. Purging is fast and quickly returns the user to a relieved state, and usually prefaces the onset of the peaking phase and so some consider it a specific mechanism.

The Risks

No drug is without risks, and Ayahuasca is no exception to this, and though Terrence McKenna quipped that the only risk is from astonishment, to go forth the potential user should be more informed than that.

First, it needs to be clarified what *risk* actually means, so things can be weighed up for the sake of practical use. For too long, "risk" has been sold as jingoism for scaremongering and sensationalism, causing damage to the subject rather than informing or elucidating.

Risk is the equation of the probability and the consequence of something with the potential to do harm. In other words, how likely it is to happen and how bad it would be if it does. Something like bungee jumping has a low risk because, despite the catastrophic consequences of an accident, the chances are very low relative to the number of jumps that happen. Flying has a similar, oft-quoted, risk profile, whilst things with high risk like BASE jumping using drugs like methamphetamine, show relatively small numbers of users compared to those who are killed or significantly damaged doing it. Simply stating something is "high risk" without defining what factors make it useless as a form of information, instantly scuttles the majority of headlines about drugs ever presented.

In this light, Ayahuasca presents as having very low risks, i.e. for a fair amount of people doing it very few are damaged *because* of it. Of course, people do have accidents related to Ayahuasca such as being bitten by scorpions, burning themselves, or falling off skateboards, but these things are not caused by the drug and can be easily removed from the equation.

The risk of psychosis being *caused* by Ayahuasca use is extremely low, which does not mean people, where it is already present, won't have the condition triggered. Chemically Ayahuasca has nothing explicitly known to trigger the condition, but where individual neurology is already compromised, there are risks that it can tip the scales in ways that are unpredictable.

A greater risk for psychosis is Ayahuasca that has been adulterated, usually with Tropane alkaloids, particularly Scopolamine from the plant Datura which is notoriously variable in potency. Datura is both poisonous and neurotoxic and the effects are disorienting, disturbing, and highly disruptive, and only exacerbated when combined with Ayahuasca's existing blend of tryptamines.

This risk is easily addressed by only having reliable and accountable sources, ideally being present when the mix is brewed so you can verify what goes into it. Similarly, using other drugs where they overlap with the Ayahuasca experience before, during, and after increases the risk of unwanted neurological and physiological effects.

Tyramine Poisoning

Ayahuasca involves Monoamine Oxidase Inhibitors, MAOIs, which immediately means caution with other things you may eat, drink, or imbibe. MAOIs counter the effect of processes in the gut that protect us from various toxins and compounds, so taking them needs to be done so carefully or the results can be very serious. Follow whatever ideology you choose with everything else, but this is the place to follow the science.

The primary risk with Ayahuasca is dietary, consuming foods that contraindicate with the drug MAOI, allowing tyramine to pass into the system, causing a toxic effect. Tyramine poisoning gets serious too fast and can last days as the system rebalances its levels of fundamental neurotransmitters. The effects range from intense headaches and a heat stroke-like condition to intracranial bleeding, seizures, and kidney failure. Tyramine poisoning will not be treated with herbal remedies or rituals and needs hospital care, to both counter the symptoms and support a system radically compromised.

This is a serious condition, with very high consequences, but thankfully very low probability if simple precautions are taken to not consume any tyramine-containing foods or fluids before, during, or after while the MAO inhibition is still active.

Not consuming cheese and beer is the most simplistic recommendation, but there is more to it than that, and some people simply fast completely to rule the whole list out, with the added benefit of emptying the stomach in anticipation of vomiting. Beyond beer and cheese, the list of foods to abstain from is significant, but all easily avoided.

Foods to avoid:

- Anything spoiled or poorly stored, especially in the tropics where it may have fermented.
- All processed meats, including bacon.
- All cheese. Some cheeses are a minimal risk but need specific identification and storage.
- Soy products including soy sauce, tofu, and miso.
- Fermented sauces like fish and oyster sauce.

- Peas and beans.
- Pickled foods including cucumber pickles and kimchi.
- Yeast products like Vegemite and sourdough.
- Over-ripened fruit, including most dry fruits.
- All alcohol.

Though not specifically due to Tyramine, people also commonly avoid caffeine, red meat, added sugar, onions and garlic, and processed fats, as much for general health and stabilizing the digestive system as any spiritual or philosophical reasons. In fact, the "Aya Diet" has emerged as a trend to keep people connected to the experience, which has many simple sensible food choices regardless of psychedelic associations.

These foods need to be avoided for a minimum of three days so they can have passed through the system, with a week commonly used to provide both a margin and to get beyond the withdrawals of diets high in caffeine, sugar, and protein.

People familiar with antidepressants may already know about and have adapted to many of these elements.

The Space

There's nothing inherently "druggy" about an Ayahuasca session, though some commercially available versions can be popular with a general drug-using subculture, and so have attributes of other things ranging from cannabis smoking to people overcoming lifestyles of damaging drug use. In itself, Ayahuasca has little of the paraphernalia and cliches of drug use, in part due to its entheogenic connections and its distance from crime.

Typically, Ayahuasca is taken in the home of either a group member or appointed guide, with space to relax and socialize, making it more like a slumber party or fondue night than a poker game or rave. No one is expected to get too uproarious or pass out, and the only things really needed are things to drink, and cushions to lay on, with even music often being unnecessary.

Unlike drugs like LSD, MDMA, and cannabis, where external stimuli play a part in the experience by projecting internal mindsets, sensory changes, and visuals onto the world, Ayahuasca is predominantly internal and not reliant on triggers. That said, it *does* have a lot of connection to voice, so talking, singing, and humming becomes powerful connectors for psychedelic phenomena to attach to.

The shared experience is not frenzied, not particularly socially intense, with a fairly equally split amount of time shared between engaging with others or in solitude. Conversation and interconnection are magnitudes of order enhanced, and expression between people is usually subtle, seemingly heightened, and minimal in emotional plays.

Sessions often happen at night as the reduced lighting helps visual phenomena arise, and contributes to the sense of intimacy that lets the rest of the world drift away. Subdued lighting, though not complete darkness, bridges the gap between eyes open and shut, where the glitches in normal consciousness can be easily located and allowed to be explored.

Despite its Amazonian origins, outdoors is not usually the ideal place for a session, unless it is somewhere comfortable and familiar, like a campground or backyard. Obviously, indigenous peoples do these things in their villages, though they usually stay fairly well within a single place, and accidents do happen with things like insect bites, thorny plants, and stepping on sharp objects. In these settings, hammocks provide a place to recline and swing, and a central fire somewhere to focus around so the shaman can oversee the dynamic of the group. Non-users tend to either stay away or keep a low presence in order to not affect the collective experience, though familiar users may be included to take part in the singing.

An Ayahuasca trip is not the place to go swimming, climbing, or playing around with fire or any other activity that will suffer from distraction or the altered perception of things like distance, touch, and social feedback. Though the connection to the environment can be profoundly felt, it should be engaged more intuitively than physically because your sense faculties have changed. Always consider the effect on the group and discuss some simple boundaries and limits, not so much for personal containment but to avert confusion and make things complicated down the road.

Nature is overwhelmingly central to the Ayahuasca experience, and for all that's recommended about avoiding risks, it should still be allowed to infuse and direct the session. Sunrises watched while on Ayahuasca will be the best in your life, and going deep into the details and organization of natural things like plants and insects is where you will find the drug at its most powerful.

Space itself changes during the Ayahuasca experience, and the way you reference things like the space around you, the distance between people, and across rooms all shift just as they do when, say, in a crowd or on the ocean. Like these examples, the change in proximity affects how you do things and identify with others, and will shift over the timeline of a trip. Rooms and spaces with an organic structure that create different zones and ways to arrange them will work better over a session than simply a four-walled cell by letting your mind play with different spatial associations, that include how you define personal space and the way others move through it.

The Dose

There are as many Ayahuasca concoctions are there are sessions, and even in the drugs homeland the content and preparation vary, though all have the basic components of a source of DMT as the psychedelic and a base of MAOI to allow it to pass actively into the system

Ayahuasca is that rare drug that requires the mixing of two additives, possibly three or more even, in order to make, which affects the already very organic nature of the components used. Other drugs come ready to imbibe, but Ayahuasca pivots as much on the ratios and the way it is prepared for its dose before you even get the matter of how much liquid volume.

In traditional settings, the dose is decided by the shaman or Ayahuscuaro, based on why you are there and the way they have prepared it, and the only way to advise on that is to be as clear and confident with your ideas and intentions and to be with a Shaman or guide who knows what they are doing. This is a deeply intimate and cultural matter, based not so much on the dose to get you the psychedelic element, but the dose needed so the other healing factors will work, such as the singing and other techniques the shaman will use.

Ayahuasca is notoriously variable in its dosage, much more so than synthetics like LSD and DMT, and even more so than psilocybin mushrooms, which depend on dried or fresh weight, mushroom size, and condition of the mushroom. Unlike fast-acting drugs where things can be topped up if the dose is found not to be enough, Ayahuasca is a one-time amount, beyond which the experience rolls out, save for the abilities of the shaman to adjust the way you are having the experience.

In most traditional settings, the liquid amount is around two hundred milliliters, which is about as much as is tolerable due to the brew's pungently astringent taste. Tasting very much as something you should not be drinking, the brain initially rejects the drinking, and it needs to be tolerated if not partially forced.

Outside of traditional use, where things are done in a modern setting and perhaps among people more focused on exploration rather than healing, the Ayahuasca concoction is usually made along a more standardized recipe or even prepackaged. This can make dosage more quantifiable, particularly if it is in a powder form, and has little to do with tweaking the ratio of the DMT component with that of the MAOIs.

Commercial preparations are arguably more palatable, having lost some of the aromatics during the drying process, though this may also affect potency and so these concoctions tend to be denser with a greater content of actual organic matter. The result is still very 'medicinal' in flavor, but no worse than many other things such as Chinese Traditional Herbs or the mescaline preparations from cacti.

It is important to distinguish between a therapeutic dose, a threshold dose, and a "heroic" dose, something that the non-traditional user needs to decide for themselves in the absence of an Ayahuascuero.

Drinking

Some sessions are very basic to the point of being "tribal" with those taking it drinking from a common pot, maybe with a common vessel that is shared around ritually. Other sessions are as urban as drinking from coffee cups filled from a pot, or even from flasks so it can be carried prepared to a location.

Ayahuasca concoctions are notoriously bad tasting, though on the scale of tryptamines are probably the least hard to get down. Compared to the astringency of most mescaline drinks, the pungently medicinal flavor of mushrooms, and the outright toxic taste of smoked DMT, Ayahuasca is usually only slightly worse than other herbal remedies.

Try to drink normally, there is no special way. Glugging too much can cause an aversion, and sipping too lightly only prolongs the event. A good medium is to drink it like it's cheap red wine or Chinese herbs, and relax back once you're done and encourage others who are there.

This part need not be particularly ceremonial, and

some are amazed at how purely functional some Ayahuasceros can be, just ladling it out like it is eggnog at Christmas. Others will make a ritual of it with offerings and incantations, and it seems the more westernized the setting, the more theater there can be.

What matters is that you take enough and have space for your own experience, which can include an accommodating atmosphere if you need to vomit or purge. Though this shouldn't hang over or define the experience, a relaxed and easy space helps to avoid any stress that comes with worrying about it.

Taking Off

The transition from a non-psychedelic state to a psychedelic one is a much-vaunted thing among all psychedelics, having a mixture of excitement, wonder, and a bit of trepidation. In many ways, it really is like taking off in a plane, as momentum builds and there is a tangible sense of forward propulsion that surprises some.

Probably a sign of the DMT, what begins as a mood shift as you relax, becomes felt as a real shift in things like gravity and spatial density. People are always on the lookout for the first signs, and with Ayahuasca, it is felt before things are seen.

Often the first reliable sign is a mild pressure all over the body like you are wearing a wetsuit or immersed in water. This is not uncomfortable and is due to slight muscular contraction, and to further the underwater association may include the urge to pop your ears.

Some people report an emerging, audible hum, that gradually rises in pitch, like a protracted version of straight DMT's signature escalating 'elevator pitch. Others hear occasional jingling or shaking of what sounds like a sort of tambourine, that seems to have no location other than behind you.

Towards the latter part of this phase, you might sense your digestive tract gurgling, as it alters how it is absorbing the brew and the blood flow from the small intestine. Most people vomit or purge towards the end of this phase, marking the entry into the next one where you are firmly in the psychedelic state.

The feeling is distinct that your mind and body are shifting their relationship, that your senses are realigning to perceive phenomena in a different way. It is exciting to go through this with a group, as each person realizes their experience is coming on, and the shared atmosphere of expectation and wonder is one of the great parts of Ayahuasca.

Being Elsewhere

The next stage is the distinct experience that you have left normal reality and that things are no longer happening along the usual course of phenomena. This begins with the novelty of things that regular reality doesn't share—like the famous image trails behind moving objects and hyper-increased sense of detail.

This is where the visual content starts, the *real* psychedelics, and the stuff that can't be initiated by placebos or fake concoctions. Arriving here means it is happening, the show has begun, and the next few hours will probably be the most interesting in your life.

Once visuals start, other senses start to chime in, building the psychedelic world that only tryptamines can. Where drugs like LSD present mostly a show made of images and ideas, Ayahuasca forms a world that has its own logic, language, and dimensions.

The mild visual novelties like auras, light trails, hyper-detail, and enhanced colors give way to actual hallucinations, like the famous vistas that take over your vision if you close your eyes or stare too long, and the replacement of your surroundings with other landscapes that feel inhibited. Sounds begin to shift, initially, as a distortion of actual noises, either incidental or provided by music or the Ayahuasceros voice, and the best shamans will know how to lay down layers of sound that fit the early stages of this evolution in your experience. You may find that you perceive a soundscape of voices or are moved along by a rhythm that has either been initiated intently or arises from the visual cues.

Peaking

For those who have not experienced Ayahuasca, the peak phase of the trip is not what you will expect. Even if you have used LSD, DMT, or Mescaline, the nature of it is very distinct. Part due to the setting Ayahuasca is usually taken in, and partly because the chemicals involved are so different, the peak of an Ayahuasca trip is as much intensity of mood as it is the intensity of hallucinations and thoughts.

If anything, the Ayahuasca peak is more about *meaning* than the peaks of other psychedelics, being more profoundly affecting than say the impressive visuals of LSD or even the intensely interesting aliveness of psilocybin. For about an hour, the depth of your connection with your psychedelic self in a psychedelic world is so immediate and apparent, that each thought makes it apparent it's a course of realization and the thoughts and actions of others seem to be more knowable, even observable. It is not hard to see where Ayahuasca's early reputation as a telepathic agent came from.

Of course, there is a hallucinatory element, something encouraged and fostered by the guide or shaman as the externalizing of your condition to meet with the condition of the setting you are in. This is often described as an archetypal thing, where forces appear to have characters and life, and that you are engaging with them with your psychedelic self that your normal self cannot do.

Peaking should be about you being able to just go with the effects, and rarely involve a total separation from this reality. Closing your eyes, of course, will mean a fully immersive and engaged experience, but opening them again should see some normalcy return though with varying degrees of overlap. Good Ayahuasceros know this stage intimately, and can determine how you are coping, and using shamanic techniques can adjust the effects with what can only be described as remarkable abilities. They know how to affect the hallucinations and perception of them by triggering your senses and sense of self, with methods ranging from blasting smoke or water, sitting close, chanting and glossolalia, and suggestion.

Without an Ayahuascero this phase is like a sequence of visions and matrix of connections between the people present that can be deeply intimate and allusive, but with a shaman present things are orders of magnitude more orchestrated, just a big band with or without a conductor. This doesn't mean control, but it does mean things have real directions, and feel more like a journey than an event. The shaman has a role that is to address some sort of matter, and takes you through the process of engaging the things that need it.

This is where the therapeutic elements are initiated, and though the real work comes in the contemplative phase that follows, it is here where the pragmatic factors arise, and that may mean some exploring. At a shamanic level, this appears to be about searching for indicators in the "other" world like ancestors, disgruntled relations in the natural world, parts of your character unrealized, or confronting deeds in the past. It is easy to be beguiled by the gorgeous visuals and bizarre hallucinations, but Ayahuasca works at its best when these things are seen for their meaning, not their novelty. Remember always the message of DMT is to not be overwhelmed, to see past the freak show, and into what they are trying to demonstrate.

Riding It

In truth, Ayahuasca doesn't really "peak" its plateaus and is a mixture of sustain effects and you're getting used to them. As immersive as things get, so too your faculties to orient yourself within it develop, and what may feel like the peak passing initially is you learning to ride it.

Beyond the peak "wow" is a stage of being inside it and looking around, and finding ways you are being affected and the extent of the stuffs' powers, because powers they really are. In this state you find that you control much more of it than you may have originally thought, far more than most literature states that this is all about loss of control.

Effectively there is *no* loss of control, it is simply a

matter of having to learn, and just as before you could ride a bicycle it all seemed like a jumble of metal parts vs uncoordinated limbs, you learn to syncopate it together with the inevitable lightbulb moment where you get it. Also like this, you get it the moment you stop forcing, when you have enough skill to get oriented and let your intuition and finer reflexes take over. Ayahuasca is the same, and the moment you position yourself inside the experience, you start to direct it to a degree seemingly not other drugs allow. DMT certainly doesn't have this level of being able to pilot it, nor does psilocybin, which though very engageable seems far too extraterrestrial to be able to know well enough to really know the process of.

Ayahuasca only becomes rideable when you fully embrace that you have taken the drug, and that this drug has opened the doors like a latch allowing you to open a window. You are not riding *the drug* per se, you are riding its effects, and all the stuff going on like visions, enhanced meanings, changed perceptions, and feelings, are the product of you and therefore yours to arrange.

The tool to use is suggestion, and to interface with the drug, as if it were its own entity with its own abilities and logic. Talk to it, ask it things, and present your own ideas, and the way it affects you will change and can be continuously tweaked. The sound and rhythm of your voice, the tone of your inference, and the reasons for your dialogue will all affect the way the Ayahuasca works. Never forget these effects arise from you, just like a woodturner uses and experiments with his tools, but the object they turn out on the lathe is the result of their imagination, observation, and skill. Entire sessions can be devoted to a subject, be it personal issues like depression and trauma, or to exploring the way the mind works when extended to things like creativity, language, and concepts.

Now this all takes time and experience to muster, and more than a small amount of courage, but as Ayahuasceros reveal an impressive degree of prowess is possible. Just as tai chi teachers can know what is coming and how to direct it from several steps ahead, the experienced Ayahuasca user can learn how to ride their experience by seeing the sequences within it. It is not a random process, instead, conforming to an organic logic, not unlike the logic of Ancient Greek or Japanese myths that are shrouded with cultural contexts.

Returning

No drug lasts forever, and eventually you will begin the journey home, usually noticed by the way the effects of the Ayahuasca become less immediate and saturated. There is a distinct feeling that you have gone as far as this session can take you, and that it is time to return, not being kicked out, but to take what you have found home.

This is the longest stage, and the better prepared for the less it feels like a winding down and the more like a time to integrate. If your peak phase was mostly about watching the psychedelic display and being awed by the strangeness then yes, it does feel like the show is coming to an end and the energy is dissipating, but if you made the peak about looking and asking then this phase fits perfectly with the process of contemplation, now that the high velocity, high saturation stuff has abated.

Only so much can be taken on board of what the peak period presents, and it take time in the world to gather the ability to get into the finer stuff, so you need to take what matters most and now tumble it over in your mind as you return, like a bit of glass being smoothed and rounded as it tumbles in the surf. This is the phase where the stuff that's too bizarre or intense can be appreciated but left for next time, and the ideas you can cope with can be built out and refined. Things will still be psychedelic enough for a few hours to keep them malleable in the mind, before they fix in normal reality as the new things to integrate.

A surprising amount of the Ayahuasca experience can come back with you, compared to DMT where very little can, LSD where you usually return with disjointed half-observations, and Psilocybin where the rewards can be hard to convey. Knowing this you can be creative with the parts of the Ayahuasca trip you choose to focus on, aware that much of their psychedelic qualities will be retained.

Examples here are things like the way forms arise from thought, where ideas and thoughts can be seen as shapes, wave patterns, disturbances of the visual field, or more explicitly as animals or entities. Obviously, it takes the drug to unleash this perception, but the idea that ideas manifest on various levels is something to consider as you come across seemingly evocative phenomena in normal life. During the return phase of the experience, when the different realities come back to form one, you get to see how the stuff you saw that was clearly Ayahuasca-induced merges into normal perception, thought sequences, and ideas.

Coming Back to Baseline

The great researchers, explorers, inventors, and flag bearers of the psychedelic community, Anne and Alexander Shulgin, described the extent of psychedelic trips in accordance to departing from and returning to a baseline of perceived normalcy. Rather than deal in totally subjective and often extremely relative metrics, they kept things simple by referencing how close to normal the individual felt.

Baseline as they define it is where there are no effects on perception, so may feel hungry, tired, or blase because they are normal features of perception that happen in everyday life regardless of any drug being taken. The key here is *perception*, so when you are reacting to the world normally again you are back, which includes normal reactions to a night without sleep, maybe a day without food (or you lost what you add by purging), and having laid around in a state of wonder for hours.

You know when you get here because the suggestive effects of the Ayahuasca have gone, and asserting ideas has no apparent effect on the way reality acts. Thoughts no longer show as colors, the amount of detail you are perceiving is back to normal, and things stay as they are no matter how long you interact with them.

The last thing to go is usually the feeling of presence, that you are somewhere that is special not just to you but to the others present and the vague notion of something beyond yourself. Ayahuasca feels like an event, not just an experience, and when you come back to baseline, the event is over and the band has left the stage.

For the distance you go with Ayahuasca, the "come down" is surprisingly benign, certainly nothing like the bleached nerves and frazzled starkness LSD can have, or the gloomy, sugar-leeched exhaustion commonly found with MDMA.

Ayahuasca leaves you tired, a bit sad that the wonder and strangeness has gone, but usually satisfied and appreciative that things have returned to predictability. As wonderful as the experience is, you can't stay there forever, and going that far into the scapes of consciousness takes energy and time to absorb. Indeed, Ayahuasca can move fast, with not enough time to grasp it all, and it can be nice to glide back to the normal world where things happen with less astonishment.

Afterwards

Stick around after, because much of what you will realize about the experience happens as normalcy seeps back in, especially the first sleep after and other firsts like eating, swimming, socializing, and sex. You don't want to be in transit or rush hour if avoidable.

The assumption runs with the theories around neuroplasticity, where it has been shown that the neurological effect stays for days, even up to two weeks after the DMT has been through your system. This makes logical sense in a way, that the DMT isn't actually leaving your brain, more than normals are returning to normal, and so do all the other chemical relationships that go with which include the beta-carbolines. Just as antidepressants containing beta-carbolines take time to enter or leave the system, so will Ayahuasca, having subtle effects as they do.

Ayahuasca is a journey and returning simply to repeat the event without integrating it is to miss the point. Every experience builds on and goes further than the ones before, and harnessing this sense of a journey puts it in context. Of course some things not addressed in one experience may be revisited in later ones, and common elements tend to present over multiple experiences, but the more you relate to it all as a journey rather than the repeating of an event like going to a baseball game, the sooner see Ayahuasca in its true expression.

A single Ayahuasca experience tends to raise more questions and ideas than it resolves, whilst also encouraging you to investigate further both through further experiences and in the rest of your life. This has no relation to addiction or habituation, nor being like an infatuation with the buzz of skydiving or roller coasters, being closer perhaps to scuba diving or dancing, where each time raises new potential and refines your abilities to take them on.

CHAPTER 5
Psychedelic Exploration

Psychedelics have as long a history of exploration as anything in the geographical realm. Perhaps going back even earlier than our first migrations out of the fertile basins of Africa, we have voyaged as far with the mind as we have climbed mountains, crossed deserts, and sailed the seas, and according to some accounts that have done both as the same thing.

Early accounts of exploration have little distinction between the journeys of the mind and across the landscape, with the Greeks and Chinese assuming that real exploration required both. Right up to the twentieth century great modern explorers like Mallory, Crowely, and Younghusband all saw their world travel as compliments to their exploration of the mind.

Ayahuasca certainly presents an entry into real exploration that most people can engage in, unlike high altitude climbing or trips to the poles, which are very expensive and take up months of time. The frontiers of the psychedelic mind are less mapped than the very places these tryptamines come from, with huge potential to join humanity to explore stuff that matters.

Exploration, of course, is a very real matter, and dabbling and dilettantism won't get you far from the shore. The depths and highs of the worlds and scapes of the mind and dimensions of consciousness demand preparation and more than a little wherewithal to take on. This is not "getting high" or tripping for the weekend, but the intent is to look into the barely known reaches of experience itself. By its very nature, these things demand ordeals and heroic doses to initiate them, like all real exploration only happening beyond the edges of what is familiar.

Intrepidation

You are meant to fear tryptamine experiences, not be terrified, but it is healthy to have your fear mechanisms triggered, in part to be wary and in part to overcome them. Fear is what defines this as something commanding respect, patience, and trust, and is usually effective at deterring those not ready for the experience.

The obvious fear is that of losing one's mind, such as some kind of psychosis or loss of control leading to injury. Decades of propaganda have played on exactly this, and like all propaganda it is misinformation and unsubstantiated hysteria, but nevertheless forms part of modern culture that has to be dealt with.

For those with no history of mental or behavioral

problems, Ayahuasca presents no obvious risks, excluding anything related to the setting of the event such as the location, conditions, people present, and attitude at the time. Properly prepared and taken in a secure environment among people who understand what is happening, it is as safe as going to a restaurant and likely safer than going to a bar.

The fear here relates mostly to entering the unknown, which is expected and healthy because it's also part of the attraction. Not unlike the anxiety and intrepidation of leaving for overseas or going out on stage, it is the sort of fear that begins to dissolve the moment things start to get going.

Like skilled mountaineers and tightrope performers, the fear never goes away; it just gets replaced with respect, knowledge, and skill, which is exactly the way to approach Ayahuasca. All the things that induce fear are usually rational and sensible, and can be addressed and resolved so you can progress safely and confidently.

Spectators, Tourists, and Explorers

Most people who visit India are not there to climb Kanchenjunga, and most people who take psychedelics don't do so to explore them.

What is often called "exploring" is analogous to taking a booked tour with a guide, and must be differentiated from actual exploration and navigating your way through uncharted territory.

It is one thing to set out with the intention to go somewhere new having the wherewithal to keep yourself safe whilst testing the waters of the unknown, and another to follow a well-established path that though bizarre and highly novel, comes back with no new insight and no more than a rant about how weird it got. This is psychedelic tourism, and of course has its own values, but is an entirely different thing to the intent to map and engage human consciousness.

Any form of exploration, be it climbing mountains or going into the "mind behind the mind" does not happen by chance or accident. Unlike misadventure, which is the following of uncontrolled events, exploration is backed up by research, hypothesis, and analysis. Part of being an explorer is the acceptance that what you see and find has value, being worthy to others who share similar ideals.

Simply to be around the Ayahuasca experience with only token use is to keep yourself from the forefront of what it can do and where it can go. Implicit in tryptamines is the draw of unique personal experience, to find your own way of navigating the psychedelic world in parallel to the experiences of others, not by following them.

In these days of fairly common Ayahuasca use,

many people are investing their energy as psychedelic tourists, more involved in commenting on the minute they have no experience of rather than forging out to find their own answers. Like package tourism to places like beach resorts and theme parks, this is useful for raising awareness and discussion, but useless for actual investigation. Podcasts, popular media articles, click bait stories by parasitic online websites, the noise generated by these mostly voyeuristic sources far outweighs any content or actual information, more diluting the useful information with bland repetition.

It is easy to avoid this by simply putting your own experience first, and building a base of experience and questioning all that you hear. Quickly most people find out that the bulk of what is being discussed on Ayahuasca and other similar things, is either mimicry or rehash of the popular protagonists of the past. Even the dissenting arguments are tired and contrived, rarely more than cherry-picked events that lack real scrutiny or suffer the rigors of research. Alarmingly similar to package tourism in its tunnel vision of the things it purports to have experience of, this sort of broadcasting over time will more limit psychedelic exploration than contribute to it.

Worse still is "psychedelic voyeurism" which is based on effectively no first hand experience but plenty of shallow reading and talk. This is the stuff that fills talk shows and news programs, and has always been the bane of serious research. Once this was a covert platform for actual users wishing to avoid scrutiny over their use of what was thoroughly illegal, but the space now has been taken up by usually well-intentioned cheerleaders, who would contribute mostly white noise and distraction.

Much of this spectator element associates Ayahuasca with a larger new age paradigm, as a catalyst for other ideologies they intersect with little rigor of thought, let alone experience. Whilst cultural fusion has its place in a comparative and syncretic way, it is no more than marketing and cheapening when the motive is to sell what goes with it or explain away the more gritty aspects.

Both the tourist and voyeuristic elements usually base their shallow perspectives in fear of confronting the actual parts of the psychedelic experience that really matters. Anyone describing their experience like a whimsical holiday or fanciful vision, is leaving out the heroic elements where the real stuff happens.

Authentic exploration of the tryptamine consciousness is as arduous as any geographical expedition and can instantly be recognized in the worlds and intentions of those who do it. Usually these types center their accounts on the things that they are confused and pragmatically stumped by, not the entertaining vistas that hint at only minimum dosages.

Always like geographical exploration, the psychedelic variety doesn't happen by accident, and those who do this are under no illusions that what they are doing involves courage and confrontation. This stuff is based on a foundation of experience and insight that can't be substituted with cliche and bluff, because the very motivation is different from the tourism that seeks only novel experience.

Psychedelic Culture

Ayahuasca is deeply embedded in its community, perhaps more so than any other drug, and part of this community is the shared knowledge of what people find and experience, going back millennia. Comparable to the societies around other forms of exploration, this network has been mapping and conjecturing on the nature and form of the experience, and anyone who goes into it is encouraged to take part.

Unlike many parallel practices, Ayahuasca is not usually kept secret, and though some groups keep low profiles for legal or philosophical reasons, books like this relating the inner details and practices are in common circulation for anyone.

The very word *psychedelic*, just like the word *drug*, carries a host of issues when it comes to talking about Ayahuasca. A problem-child since its early use in the mid-twentieth century among maverick researchers, it soon hit popular culture as a fundamental meme of the hippie and countercultures. Coupled to LSD it made cultural sense, being products of post-war technology and consumerism, but applied to ancient entheogens like Ayahuasca and peyote that have long histories in their own languages, it subject them to the same cliches and juvenile trends that perfectly suited LSD.

"Psychedelic" massively understates Ayahuascas nuances and overwhelming cultural aspects, making it sound like a lurid spectacle of kaleidoscopes and throbbing synthesizers in the way LSD is portrayed. It implies *wowserism* and a certain euphoric entertainment, but fails to convey the actual nature of Ayahuasca in all its complexity and intimateness.

But, as those who have been here before have all found, it's the only word we have in a language rich in words to describe drunkenness and soporifics, but contributes so little to the discussion of approaching the mind and behavior in this way. We may think of the heyday of psychedelics as being the 1960s, a quaint though naively misguided era that we grew out of once the novelty subsided, but that's not what really happened. Whilst true, the media frenzy turned elsewhere and the bands that broadcast the LSD message moved on as did the public's tastes, psychedelic drug use and exploration continued, with several resurgences since. Once the media lost interest, psychedelics could go about their own evolution largely ignored, and it is a testimony to popular hysteria that the once-predicted societal crash from using these things never came. For all the doomsday predictions at the start, unabated psychedelic use has continued, and *despite* the interventions of ill-adapted legal systems, it has become safer and more acceptable over time. Left alone, in the hands of users, psychedelics became a force for good—something unthinkable in half a century ago when they were cast as the most dangerous threat to society.

Following the loss of interest in psychedelics in the early 1970s, they became an unfashionable trend, kept alive by overgrown drop outs and hippies clinging to nostalgia. Mescaline went on its journey to becoming recognized for its entheogenic value, and psilocybin slowly built a grassroots base as people discovered ways to grow them themselves. Entheogens emerged as where the psychedelic frontier was going now that LSD was relegated to little more than an undergraduate novelty, and the spotlights of contemporary culture turned to things like heroin chic, heavy metal on stimulants, and heartland rock that took people back to the good old days of getting drunk.

Slowly stirring beneath the surface, as the media looked for the next drug hysteria, was the incubating scene around MDMA that had escaped its experimental use in psychotherapy. Just as the frenzy over freebased cocaine was peaking, MDMA branded as "ecstasy" hit the mainstream, often billed as 'the second summer of love'.

Very much a psychedelic in its own right, MDMA nevertheless piggy-backed other psychedelics in with it, with LSD being the top selling street drug since the early 1970s according to some think tanks. Changes in globalization such as flights, politics, and immigration, also meant more people were traveling to places where things like Ayahuasca and psilocybin mushrooms were being used.

The explosion of "rave culture" included the birth of the internet, with a big crossover of users in what became called the cyberpunk culture, and at the core of it were the remnants of the old guard from the sixties, plus a host of new figure heads voicing stuff the sixties couldn't ever have dreamed of. "Psychedelic" now included computers, what had once been the enemy of the counterculture, and digital centers were the new centers of psychedelic culture that included the boom in self-publishing.

People like Terence McKenna had for years been forced to use lo-fi, low circulation media to broadcast the message about entheogens for the user, bridging the gap between the enthusiastic user and the scientific researchers who were at polar ends of the credibility spectrum. Now, self-publishing and websites are getting quality information disseminated at low cost, fueling a wave of culture that had Ayahuasca central to it.

This time round things were less sensational, the facts were too good, and rather than revolutionaries as the spokespeople there were researchers and explorers that fitted the internet's geek culture. Instead of being all lumped together as a wall of societal panic, psychedelics were—for the first time in western history since the Elysian Mysteries of Ancient Greece—being looked at for their benefits.

Ayahuasca especially was given respect, by having no baggage from the hippie era and a multicultural presence that was appreciated by a modern world shrugging off its chauvinistic past. Psychedelics have a natural tendency to rise to the top of the intelligentsia in society if allowed, and Ayahuasca fitted a space that combined exploration, culture, travel, and Western Societies thirst for personal improvement that had been pushed as a norm by generations raised on pharmaceuticals.

In the western mind, *everybody* had some kind of personality disorder; be it ADHD, regressive memories, PTSD, or depression, which made chemical correction both normal and a point of suspicion. Undoubtedly, some people needed tweaking or reorganizing with drugs that affected brain chemistry, but the companies that made and prescribed them seemed a little too eager to have people using them. This first generation to go through school laced together with drugs, graduated knowing more about how their brains worked than any collective age group before, emboldening them for drug use as adults for both therapy and fun. The smart ones realized the same names on their medications were similar to what was purportedly in Ayahuasca, and with Latin America now emerging from its politically unsavory paste, a few weeks backpacking that included a search for an Ayahuascero became the thing to do.

Now Ayahuasca exists as a quasi-legitimate thing to pursue, and rather than being attacked by the media as a force of the devil, is routinely trivialized to fit whatever agenda the outlet presents. Late-comers to the subject align it with new age and fashionista trends such as kale and wheatgrass, as much as a way to discredit the users as anything to do with the drug itself. To many the idea of looking beyond the narrow tunnel of their own small worldview is somehow sinister, and nothing sells news like the blend of ignorance and fear.

Ayahuasca Tourism

Not long ago, traveling to parts of the Amazon to partake in an Ayahuasca session was a major affair involving arduous travel through often unstable areas, obscure processes for finding societies that used it openly, luck, and a lot of trust in people who held all the cards for the thing you were looking for. That it was outlawed in most places—like the illegalization of anything—pushed it underground or into remote areas where outsiders were not always welcome. Reports surfaced of people being conned, ripped off, extorted, and even poisoned.

Ayahuasca may be a legal gray area in some places, but it is firmly illegal in others in the highest category of drugs considered harmful and useless imposed by the United Nations, which among other avenues has spawned purveyors who offer it in international waters. Often in parallel with Ibogaine addiction treatments, these services take place on boats off the coast of some major cities, in an atmosphere not ignorant of the pirate radio stations of the late 1960s.

Nowadays, opportunities to travel to take Ayahuasca, combining the ease of international flights with the availability of the drug, remove much of the risk associated with doing it where it is strictly outlawed. Some countries in South America have made it legal altogether for localized use and thus opened up an entire sector of tourism, whilst in places with relaxed enforcement elsewhere offer private trips that can include boats in international waters.

Some of these places offer the actual shamanic experience, very similar to traditional use in as much authentic context as possible. Obviously, these tend to happen in local languages and by local standards, so are outside the scope of some people, but adapted versions exist that still include most of the elements.

It *is* still tourism though, which doesn't always attract the best of any society, and hustlers, third parties, and scammers exist. Locating and engaging sessions at the degree of authenticity a traveler requires is not always straightforward, and is something that changes year by year as the scene and places evolve.

Beyond actual Amazonian locations, the providers of Ayahuasca sessions dramatically change, along a spectrum of experiences that range from very close to the traditional to very little like it. Some are unapologetic, instead exploring Ayahuasca for its other potentials where traditions are held separate, and others are basically theater and a corny mock version of a fantasy. In between are a whole array of styles, associated often with local views on such things, where some places in Eastern Europe using it along with Ibogaine as part of a long history for treating addiction, and places in Australia using it to try and find an analog for things the indigenous cultures may have had.

As a reason to travel, it is not a bad one, though all the usual attributes around travel still also apply, including an understanding of what happens if you come afoul of local laws. Depending on the destination's view on such things, the consequences could be a fine, expulsion, or serious time in jail. Like always, as the traveler, it is *your* job to know this as pleading ignorance is never a defense in the eyes of a judiciary. This should form part of your research when looking for and booking these things, and any decent provider will have clear and genuinely informative answers. If not, ignore them.

Microdosing

The most exposure psychedelics get in the mainstream press is in relation to microdosing. The idea that these drugs can be taken in "subthreshold" amounts that infer some of their benefits without the actual psychedelic experience. Popular media has been quick to pick up on this story as a good overlap of content, that combines an attention-grabbing headline with some quasi-science and a trendsetting presence.

Whilst there is some weight to the idea, it is rarely what the popular media covers, with far more being left out and overlooked than anything useful being covered. News site stories are not the platform suitable for this sort of information in any real quality, doing more to raise awareness and define a demographic of interest than to inform anyone how to do it.

Of all the psychedelics, Ayahuasca lends itself among the least functional to use, having so many variables and organic attributes to make it unreliable at such doses. Half the issue with microdosing is that the object is to not really notice any effects, instantly calling into question the whole concept even with pharmaceutical grade compounds, let alone something as variable as Ayahuasca that is taken in liquid form as a fundamental element.

Stripping the psychedelic ordeal from the experience, any traditional user will tell you it renders the entire thing pointless, because as we have said many times before, it is not the drug itself that does any healing. The western pharmacological view is of course different, being well aware of the actions of the beta-carbolines and other tryptamines and the relation to neurotransmitters, though even in this case the amounts are very low compared to what is found in commonly available medications.

Where something like psilocybin may have a microdosing effect, being used at about 6% of the usual full dose, and much easier to determine dosage simply because it doesn't have the two-part recipe nor the balance of multiple separate physiological processes in several independent parts of the metabolism.

Placebo plays a real role in any microdosing process, even when the action of the drug is well-defined and known to be acting. Indeed, the placebo effect is a factor in *any* psychedelic experience, even the most blatant ones, simply because suggestion, nuance, and hyper attention to detail is at the root of the whole thing.

At a psychedelic level this may not matter, but at a physiological one where chemical influences are integral it does, and if the reasons for microdosing relate to the actions and balances of quantifiable neurotransmitters then just thinking you are getting the effects may be more of a problem than solution.

All this makes Pharmahuasca a better option, though still fails to address the shamanic aspect of the experience around it where the real changes are made either by supernatural or behavioral actions.

CHAPTER 6
The Psychedelic Lifestyle

Life is better with psychedelics on the table, and even if you have no urge to use them, they form a whole world to think about just like art, travel, history, and cooking. You don't have to be a psychedelic user to appreciate them just as you don't have to paint to go into a gallery or cook to go into a restaurant, and simply enjoying their presence in the world and the curious things that come with it makes you to some degree psychedelic and part of the community.

Even as a psychedelic user, this by no means having to use them often, or even regularly, with the majority of people using entheogens doing so over years rather than days. The weekend raver who lives along a constant curve of use and waiting is not at all the standard of the psychedelic lifestyle, nor are most of the other stereotypes an uninformed media would have you believe.

Should You Try Ayahuasca?

Without avoiding the question, this is better asked

as should you *not* try Ayahuasca? because the first way of phrasing it immediately frames both the drug and the experience as something alien and without reason.

As weird and novel as the Ayahuasca experience can be, it is not a complete anomaly in life that is so far outside common experience that it needs to be treated as unapproachable. Neither the nature of the pharmacology nor the nature of the experience is radically at odds with most people's lives, and viewed this way is seen to be less invasive or hazardous as getting drunk or taking tranquilizers or painkillers.

Ayahuasca runs effectively with no risk of addiction—indeed sometimes being the panacea or cure for it===so runs no risk in itself of kickstarting an antisocial habit. Unlike common recreational drugs such as MDMA, most stimulants, and cannabis, the conditions for Ayahuasca don't present regularly such as the predictability of weekends, making almost no casual scene within which to get carried away.

Even more so than psilocybin, which overlaps a lot with recreational use, Ayahuasca tends to shrug it off due to the profound nature of the experience, feeling more like an expedition or adventure than a titillation or buzz. Just as few people embark on serious mountaineering or caving trips more than a few times a year, if that, Ayahuasca doesn't instill the urge to do it at every given opportunity. Perhaps the best comparison is with straight DMT itself, which is an experience so stunning and so thought-provoking, that it takes time to assimilate upon which the idea of doing it again is built.

Taking Ayahuasca doesn't shift your ability in society, so there is no need to take on a different lifestyle that affects things like eating and sleeping. Once over what is usually a night without sleep and much eating, you return to normal quickly, aside from the new ideas you have found.

To *not* try Ayahuasca is to not step through a door that has been with us as long as there has been history, through which many have been before and all have returned better than when they left. There are no homes broken by Ayahuasca, or violent crimes, or deprivation that goes with it, only a culture of contemplation and insight that is embedded in our history. Wars have not been fought because of it, and until the last century laws have left it alone, meaning that by trying it you are not part of the negative side of human history or dabbling in something with sinister associations.

Relative to other drugs that a large proportion of people carve out whole aspects of their lives to cater to, Ayahuasca

Now none of this is to say you *should* try Ayahuasca. Instead, it is to say most people need not avoid or discount it, which leaves the space for a small percentage that is best leaving it alone. At its root, Ayahuasca is still neurologically active chemicals acting on both the digestive tract and brain, so people with problems in either should be clear what they are dealing with first.

Getting a Supply

Ayahuasca is not cannabis or even cocaine, where everybody knows somebody, and it is somewhere at most parties. One of the best things about it is that it doesn't follow the strictures of organized crime, so though probably illegal in your location, probably won't involve other activities like scum bag dealers, gangs, traffickers, or bad police.

Outside of the Amazon forests and a handful of very rare places where cultivated, getting Banisteriopsis Caapi in its raw form is very difficult, taking several years to grow and requiring a significant amount. Sources abound claiming to sell cuttings and cultivars, but this is a long game that requires the right conditions and know-how.

Psychotria Viridis, on the other hand, is easily found and easily grown with quick results. Apart from its contribution to psychedelic lore it is an unassuming shrub that can be grown like any other tropical pot plant, and harvested without killing it, and produces more plants easily from cuttings and grafts.

Unlike cannabis, which is usually grown under

highly unnatural conditions in order to force production, neither Banisteriopsis nor Psychotria take well to intensive commercial production.

Both plants are available as prepared material, individually so as to avoid much of the legal matters, with both being sold as herbal tea mixtures, incense, or new age accouterments similar to crystals or sage. Informed sellers may have recommendations, though may not sell more than a single item together, and may have a process for duty of care to make sure you know what you are dealing with.

Prepared Ayahuasca powders are available online, with varying degrees of legality, quality, and potency. These powders come from enterprising growers, usually through an intermediary cottage industry that knows what they are doing but may lack quality control. These things will never come with instructions or approval for consumption, and beyond laws pertaining to the selling and shipping of such things will also be governed by mundane rules around ordering plant material.

Other sources of beta-carbolines and DMT exist, though usually not easily in the same place. Variants of mimosa in the form of wattle trees are ornamentals commonly found, and several types of pasture grasses can be grown from seed as easily as wheatgrass. Both require their own methods of extraction and preparation and have a similar result, though there is a clear distinction with Amazonian Ayahuasca that seems linked to the traditions of the plants used.

Beta-carbolines from Syrian Rue for example, though being chemically the same, produce an experience that is noticeably more geometric, and seems to be reflected in the patterns, textures, and atmosphere of Persia and Byzantium. How this works is open to interpretation, and may simply be a suggestion in the same way so much else is suggestible with tryptamines, or may be a more fundamental thing going the other way where what we see of those cultures has this as its origin. Similarly DMT from Australian acacia origins has a very different quality to Psychotria, again like Beta-Carbolines from Asia Minor, having qualities of the indigenous culture. It is entirely possible that these acacian tryptamines have even a longer entheogenic history than the Amazonian ones, and the experience is explicitly cave-like echoing the weathering of sandstone, with the organic colors and patterns of indigenous Australian art that already has a very "tryptamine" quality.

These concoctions provide no less a psychedelic experience, but do lack the shamanic guidance of the Amazonian version, being either unknown, hidden, or lost to colonization. They provide usually legal sources from plants that have other uses and reputations, Australia famously not being able to outlaw one—despite trying—because it is the country's national emblem.

Never decide to bring any home with you if you visit indigenous areas. Removing indigenous plants in itself is unethical, and to most destinations it becomes trafficking with all the personal and legal aspects that go with it, including how it reflects on your community.

Plants are still plants and can harbor unwanted insects and molds, things that customs take very seriously even if there's no flagging over the use as a psychedelic. Any laws about use, no matter how benign, will be amplified by magnitudes when combined with trafficking across borders. Ayahuasca may be a low risk and even beneficial thing in the eyes of science, but in the eyes of the law it can be prosecuted just like heroin and methamphetamine, including intent to supply.

Pharmahuasca comes as either two components, both pharmaceutically produced, which is not a legal issue with beta-carbolines but almost always means illegally for DMT, or it comes premixed as a low grade pharmaceutical that could have untrustworthy origins. Sources for both are misappropriated labs, usually after hours or in industrial companies, and though intentions might be fine the skill level may not be, nor the grade of the set up and sanitation of operation. Pharmahuasca can easily be substituted with cheaper, more easily available psychedelics like LSD, MDMA, or Mescaline, which themselves are regularly adulterated with amphetamines, opioids, and tranquilizers.

As attractive as the idea of Pharmahuasca is, it needs access to quality supply that is far removed from ordering herbal teas, taking cuttings, or growing shrubs on your patio. Going this route requires care and certain connections, without which it starts to run counter to the ethics of Ayahuasca fast, which include responsibility and accountability for your actions and your place in your community.

Ayahuasca Groups

Ayahuasca is by its very nature a group thing. It is no stretch to hear about lone trips on psilocybin and LSD, and DMT is a very solo thing apart from the overwhelmingly crowded and busy place it takes you to, but when it comes to Ayahuasca, it is hard to imagine it minus the community element.

Embedded in the experience is the factor that it is the group itself that forms the narrative, and from the traditional shamanic version to the contemporary pharmahuasca one, the group forms what defines how things go. The brewing, the shared space, the concept of being guided, and the interactions with others, all set the group element even before the role of a shaman is included. Many Ayahuasca sessions take place, with groups now found everywhere, with no shaman role present but still grounded in the dynamic of a group.

Churches form a large part of the Ayahuasca community, and though not often part of what those exploring the drug interact with, account for the largest number of users and maybe even the largest organized psychedelic community there is. Ayahuasca churches range from ones continuing the shamanic tradition, to others that combine it with Christian beliefs, and neo-pagan groups that have invented their own system and are seeking legitimacy.

Like any church, organizations that are legitimate have structures, hierarchies, and doctrines, and though Ayahuasca is central to it, there are all the other aspects shared with every organization. These groups are not usually casual and open to outsiders.

Something Ayahuasca *doesn't* seem to adhere to when it comes to group experience is a place in rave culture. Where every other psychedelic is central to the music, atmosphere, flow of the event, Ayahuasca is rarely present even if the music alludes to it as in the case of several well-known music producers.

Ayahuasca seems to connect to the intimacy of a group and not the presence of one, with the heaving, massively moving and multifarious nature of a rave not being what Ayahuasca functions well with. Ayahuasca is relatively analog and low-energy compared to something like LSD, and though it certainly has the facility for movement and dancing, it doesn't push it for hours in the highly stimulated way that other psychedelics do.

This does not mean it cannot be used alone, but it does mean the usual parameters of solo psychedelic use apply differently, shifting expectations, planning, and conduct. Any psychedelic used alone is vastly different to when used with a group, with Ayahuasca perhaps being the most so. Even in a group, things like LSD, psilocybin, and DMT are intensely personal, but Ayahuasca by nature is very much a socially-oriented thing. Vomiting alone whilst on the verge of the Ayahuasca breakthrough is not the stuff for the inexperienced, uncommitted, or easily perturbed.

Beyond all the cautions and advisories, solo psychedelic use can be a beautiful experience that goes to places impossible to go to otherwise, and may be the true mark of the real shaman or explorer.

Ayahuasca and Teenagers

Teenagers are attracted to drugs and high-intensity experiences like moths to a flame, and there are two ways to deal with this; with education or without.

There is no prize for picking which is the better way.

The problem with education is it is based on the intentions, integrity, and knowledge of the teacher, and for generations now we have seen drug education—let alone in psychedelics specifically—mostly fail. Indeed, it is a testament to the resourcefulness of our teenagers that despite our best and most well-funded efforts to coerce, intimidate, and lie to our youth, they have managed a level of damage control that keeps seeing them through.

Psychedelic education was not helped by the rampant advocation of people like Timothy Leary, who despite a brilliant intelligence and good intentions was too easy to target by those who oppose such things, effectively hobbling education and research into these things for decades to come. This campaign continues with no discussion of psychedelics possible without mention of his name, though always without informed context as the caricature of his legacy lives on.

Drugs historically have formed part of an initiation into adulthood, sometimes as ordeals to be survived, other times as a way of defining adult spaces that the imbibing of certain drugs grants one entry. Many initiating ordeals in general involve acute acts of courage and tolerance, and it is interesting to note that societies that use psychedelics tend not to also use more extreme initiations like body modification, violence, and trauma.

The growing and reorganizing neurology of a teenager is already so bombarded with signals that the introduction of something as profound as Ayahuasca needs to be considered seriously. Despite the best efforts of industry to cast all teenagers as being similar, this is clearly not true, but the chances are still that what they see about drugs will be aimed at them this way.

Our children are as stupid as we allow them to be, and it is unhealthy for society to deny something to one due to the ignorance or maturity of another. In many cases, teenagers are better informed than their parents, or at least more up to date as to the parameters of something like Ayahuasca in society.

Two decades ago, any teenager aware of Ayahuasca probably knew it from obscure books or maybe interested parents. Now, Ayahuasca is part of common experience, with magnitudes more discussion and acceptability.

In traditional use, Ayahuasca is not reserved for adults, and just like any strong medicine is used cautiously with anyone requiring its benefits. Because it is usually associated with aspects of health that the traditional society relates with things not recognized in our culture—namely magic, psychic interference, influence of ancestors etc—Ayahuasca tends to become more relevant as a child matures into a society, and so its use on actual infants is mostly token. In these cases only tiny amounts are given, under the idea that as always it is the setting that achieves any benefits not the drug itself, so any Ayahuasca actually consumed is a minor part of the process and the singing and other practices still take place.

Studies into adolescents who have grown up with Ayahuasca use in contemporary Brazil show they are no more affected by either social or physiological ills than their non-using peers. If anything, due to the Ayahuasca being used in a traditional context with family and cultural proximity, these individuals may be better equipped as positive society members considering the often problematic issues that revolve around indigenous people in modern Brazil.

Indeed, it can be assumed that almost any adult in a traditional Ayahuasca-using society had the experience as part of their youth, as did innumerable generations that came before, and thus their entire society is a reflection of what happens. If anything Ayahuasca use among traditional youth has *decreased* with westernization, possibly being replaced with other things like alcohol, cannabis, cocaine, and other drugs, that contribute to the corrupted state many traditional Amazonian people live in today.

So should our kids have Ayahuasca made available to them? The answer is very much dependent on the context of the world around them, including the way their parents and families relate to the drug, to the law, and to the reasons why they would use it, and the 50% of the equation of what happens if they *don't* have access to it.

Banning and containing any drug is the best way to attract both the youth of any society and the criminal element that preys upon them, especially within the subcultures of ethnic, economic, educational, and outsider groups. Decades of data, plus most people's raw experience, show the way drugs ravage these demographic groups and the knock-on effects to everyone else.

A healthy paradigm for youth Ayahuasca use would prioritize the distancing from criminal elements, that includes the *making* of criminals of anybody who uses it. Ideally, it would keep its value as a healing tool, which includes the interaction with responsible guides and not framing them as drug dealers, though the aspects explained by modern medicine would be clarified such as the effects of MAOIs as mood regulators.

There is the obvious element of the way Ayahuasca intersects with diet, importantly anything containing tyramine, which is a whole different paradigm in urban western society than it is in agrarian Peru and can have serious consequences. Already we have seen the way MDMA was misunderstood in the context of modern diet when it surged to popularity in the 1980s, and the casualties of that era, though not specifically due to MDMA, have been leveraged since by groups with anti-drug agendas.

A truly responsible society would present

Ayahuasca to its curious youth as a way to orient them towards adulthood that is a mature alternative to the random and exploited drug culture they already face. Once accepted that all modern teenagers will be faced with drug use at some point and that some will make bad choices simply because of peer pressure and misinformation, Ayahuasca can be part of the landscape as a responsible option, with responsible adults involved and a positive platform around it.

Ayahuasca should be seen in its traditional context as a device for exploration and personal growth—something that has been maintained fairly well so far. Anything that reduces reliance on self-medicating with products offered by organized crime syndicates and forced underground by massively disproportionate legislation is a good thing for our kids.

AYAHUASCA AND THE FREE CITIZEN

Should anyone stop you from trying Ayahuasca?

The simple answer is in general no, because it offers little risk to most people, and those who may find complications with it likely already know this.

The longer answer is "it depends" and is based on how you see the world and yourself in it. Ayahuasca has the potential to significantly change the way you think about things, and you need to be fine with the results of that.

Ayahuasca does not fit into every society and social group, and despite psychedelic tryptamines being as old as culture itself, they have to be largely sidelined and overlooked for enough of history that they don't always adhere to social narratives.

We have the inalienable right to be healthy. Not all drugs are created equal, and the use of some that have a large potential for abuse and negative behavior are understandably needing control. Ayahuasca is not one of those drugs.

In some circles, Ayahuasca runs counter to what

people consider acceptable, almost always due to either misunderstanding about what it is, or because of a deep-seated distrust or taboo about exploring and understanding your own brain. Many social groups consider this to be something that must only be done *to you* by ordained or decreed experts such as doctors or a clergy, rather than something you can do *for yourself* as the one having and directing the experience.

Indeed, some drugs do need special administration because they can be harmful in tiny increments or because they have contraindications that are complex and critical, but again, Ayahuasca is not one of these drugs.

How Ayahuasca fits with other aspects of your life that are spiritual, religious, or ideological all depends on how much personal freedom, exploration, and responsibility those other aspects encourage. Where these attributes are held very highly with the use of Ayahuasca, being known as the things that bring value and integrity to the experience, some other ideologies don't share this. In which case the individual must decide for themselves.

CONCLUSION

Coming to Ayahuasca is deciding to take up traveling, or if you already travel, finding there is a whole continent you have been unaware of. What is out there is vast, with a lifetime or more worth of exploring, and like any new destination, informs your view of everything else.

In many ways, Ayahuasca is as "out there" as it is "in here," forming a fluid conduit between your thinking and your world. Where so much of life is the process and turmoil of trying to align these things, Ayahuasca is a rare—perhaps unique—connection between both.

In this respect, Ayahuasca puts you in the center of the journey, but not you the protagonist, instead you the conduit. Rather than living as just the focus of your life, you realize what runs through you, that you inhabit interconnected worlds, and that who you are here is only one version of yourself.

As we have discussed, Ayahuasca is a very real tool for a very real experience that can change who you are in this one by growth and exploration of another. Like the traveler who brings home the lessons and insights of their time away, so it is with Ayahuasca and what you do when you take it.

The culture and extent of the Ayahuasca world is far greater than the uninitiated can know, and even the most ardent and courageous explorers have only brought back an inkling of what is going on there. We know it is real, that people are accepted, that as different as it all appears, there are many connections, and that time spent experiencing it is positive and safe. We know that some traditions have been familiar with this for millenia, centuries longer than the ideologies and traditions that make up our civilization, and have an accumulated knowledge unbroken across hundreds of generations with a body of information we are beginning to understand. Modern science is adding to the picture, though requiring many updates and rethinks to do so, but is coming to the realization that much of this world is as the traditional users say.

For all this, to go into Ayahuasca is not to join a strange cult, go native, or be brainwashed. If anything, it is the opposite and the antidote for those things. The pharmacology, rites, and nature of the experience is one that shrugs off destructive behavior, and has a powerful ability to free up even the most calcified of minds.

In a world that can appear to be speeding towards pointlessness, desperation, incoherence, and loss, Ayahuasca allows a perspective big enough to navigate your place in it all. It won't answer your trivialities or proof you from consequence, but it plugs into a mindset that widens your ability to see. Science confirms that these are not ordinary drugs, that the tryptamine psychedelics don't act the same way that the drugs that confuse and addict us do. These are the same chemicals upon which the brain itself runs, and expertly using them allows a level of thought to match many of our problems.

Set Out

The goal of this book has been to prepare you, to provide what you need for the Ayahuasca experience. Like a sailor preparing for sea, what you have here is a set of maps and a theodolite to navigate by, not just to follow in the footsteps of others but to find new things yourself.

What lies ahead is a mix of science, myth, hearsay, and hard facts and you need your wits about you, your eyes open and your boots on. As positive and awe-inspiring as Ayahuasca will be, it needs courage and confidence and won't tolerate fools. Things are not what they seem, and what they seem to be is already out on the edge of normal experience, and for the modern explorer is every bit as demanding as an expedition anywhere.

Our world needs more explorers, those with the courage to go further and look at things in new ways, and to bring back reports that can be trusted and used. You may have missed your chance in the great eras of travel, but an emerging era of exploring the mind is underway that you can decide to join, or not.

For the person new to all this, from here it all looks daunting, massive, distant, and impenetrable, and indeed it is, and those qualities never leave. What does change is who you are, as you build your experience and confidence, continuously being met by the Ayahuasca as your ability grows.

SUBSCRIBE TO SOFIA VISCONTI

Greetings!

As a subscriber, you will receive a **Free Gift** + you will be the first to hear about new books, articles and more exclusives **just for you.**

Simply scan the qr code to join.

REFERENCES

Aronson, J. K. (2014). Ayahuasca - an overview | ScienceDirect Topics. Www.sciencedirect.com.

Bouso, J. C., Andión, Ó., Sarris, J. J., Scheidegger, M., Tófoli, L. F., Opaleye, E. S., Schubert, V., & Perkins, D. (2022). Adverse effects of ayahuasca: Results from the Global Ayahuasca Survey. PLOS Global Public Health, 2(11), e0000438.

Burroughs, W. S., & Ginsberg, A. (1975). The Yage Letters.. City Lights Publishers.

Carbonaro, T. M., & Gatch, M. B. (2016). Neuropharmacology of N,N-dimethyltryptamine. Brain Research Bulletin, 126, 74–88. https://doi.org/10.1016/j.brainresbull.2016.04.016

Colaço, C. S., Alves, S. S., Nolli, L. M., Pinheiro, W. O., de Oliveira, D. G. R., Santos, B. W. L., Pic-Taylor, A., Mortari, M. R., & Caldas, E. D. (2020). Toxicity of ayahuasca after 28 days daily exposure and effects on monoamines and brain-derived neurotrophic factor (BDNF) in brain of Wistar rats. Metabolic Brain Disease, 35(5), 739–751.

Davis, A. K., So, S., Lancelotta, R., Barsuglia, J. P., & Griffiths, R. R. (2019). 5-methoxy-N,N-dimethyltryptamine (5-MeO-DMT) used in a naturalistic group setting is associated with unintended improvements in depression and anxiety. The American Journal of Drug and Alcohol Abuse, 45(2), 161–169.

de Rios, M. D., Grob, C. S., Lopez, E., da Silviera, D. X., Alonso, L. K., & Doering-Silveira, E. (2005). Ayahuasca in Adolescence: Qualitative Results. Journal of Psychoactive Drugs, 37(2), 135–139.

de Vos, C. M. H., Mason, N. L., & Kuypers, K. P. C. (2021). Psychedelics and Neuroplasticity: A Systematic Review Unraveling the Biological Underpinnings of Psychedelics. Frontiers in Psychiatry, 12.

dos Santos, R. G., Grasa, E., Valle, M., Ballester, M. R., Bouso, J. C., Nomdedéu, J. F., Homs, R., Barbanoj, M. J., & Riba, J. (2011). Pharmacology of ayahuasca administered in two repeated doses. Psychopharmacology, 219(4), 1039–1053.

Feingold, D., & Weinstein, A. (2020). Cannabis and Depression. Cannabinoids and Neuropsychiatric Disorders, 67–80.

Frecska, E., Szabo, A., Winkelman, M. J., Luna, L. E., & McKenna, D. J. (2013). A possibly sigma-1 receptor mediated role of dimethyltryptamine in tissue protection, regeneration, and immunity. Journal of Neural Transmission (Vienna, Austria : 1996), 120(9), 1295–1303.

Germonpré, M. (n.d.). Fossil bear bones in the Belgian Upper Palaeolithic: the possibility of a proto-bear ceremonialism. Www.academia.edu. Retrieved November 24, 2022, from

Halberstadt, A. L. (2016). Behavioral and pharmacokinetic interactions between monoamine oxidase inhibitors and the hallucinogen 5-methoxy-N,N-dimethyltryptamine. Pharmacology Biochemistry and Behavior, 143, 1–10.

Inserra, A. (2018). Hypothesis: The Psychedelic Ayahuasca Heals Traumatic Memories via a Sigma 1 Receptor-Mediated Epigenetic-Mnemonic Process. Frontiers in Pharmacology, 9.

Jiménez-Garrido, D. F., Gómez-Sousa, M., Ona, G., Dos Santos, R. G., Hallak, J. E. C., Alcázar-Córcoles, M. Á., & Bouso, J. C. (2020). Effects of ayahuasca on mental health and quality of life in naïve users: A longitudinal and cross-sectional study combination. Scientific Reports, 10(1).

Labate, B. C. (2011). Consumption of Ayahuasca by Children and Pregnant Women: Medical Controversies and Religious Perspectives. Journal of Psychoactive Drugs, 43(1), 27–35.

Labate, B. C., & Cavnar, C. (2014). The Therapeutic Use of Ayahuasca (B. C. Labate & C. Cavnar, Eds.). Springer Berlin Heidelberg.

Leary, T. (2000). Change Your Brain. In Google Books. Ronin

Publishing.

Lombardo, U., Iriarte, J., Hilbert, L., Ruiz-Pérez, J., Capriles, J. M., & Veit, H. (2020). Early Holocene crop cultivation and landscape modification in Amazonia. Nature, 581(7807), 190–193.

Ly, C., Greb, A. C., Cameron, L. P., Wong, J. M., Barragan, E. V., Wilson, P. C., Burbach, K. F., Soltanzadeh Zarandi, S., Sood, A., Paddy, M. R., Duim, W. C., Dennis, M. Y., McAllister, A. K., Ori-McKenney, K. M., Gray, J. A., & Olson, D. E. (2018). Psychedelics Promote Structural and Functional Neural Plasticity. Cell Reports, 23(11), 3170–3182.

McKenna, D. J., Towers, G. H. N., & Abbot, F. (2022). McKenna, Dennis J., G. H. N. Towers, and F. Abbot. "Monoamine Oxidase Inhibitors in South American Hallucinogenic Plants: Tryptamine and beta-Carboline Constituents of Ayahuasca," Journal of Ethnopharmacology. Vol. 10 (photocopy), 1984 | Archives and Special Collections. Purdue.edu.

McKenna, T. K. (1993). Food of the Gods: The Search for the Original Tree of Knowledge : a Radical History of Plants, Drugs, and Human Evolution. Bantam Books.

Morales-Garcia, J. A., Calleja-Conde, J., Lopez-Moreno, J. A., Alonso-Gil, S., Sanz-SanCristobal, M., Riba, J., & Perez-Castillo, A. (2020). N,N-dimethyltryptamine compound found in the hallucinogenic tea ayahuasca, regulates adult neurogenesis in vitro and in vivo. Translational Psychiatry, 10(1), 1–14.

Ott, J. (1999). Pharmahuasca: Human Pharmacology of Oral DMT Plus Harmine. Journal of Psychoactive Drugs, 31(2), 171–177.

Palhano-Fontes, F., Barreto, D., Onias, H., Andrade, K. C., Novaes, M. M., Pessoa, J. A., Mota-Rolim, S. A., Osório, F. L., Sanches, R., dos Santos, R. G., Tófoli, L. F., de Oliveira Silveira, G., Yonamine, M., Riba, J., Santos, F. R., Silva-Junior, A. A., Alchieri, J. C., Galvão-Coelho, N. L., Lobão-Soares, B., & Hallak, J. E. C. (2018). Rapid antidepressant effects of the psychedelic ayahuasca in treatment-resistant depression: a randomized placebo-controlled trial. Psychological Medicine, 49(4), 655–663.

Pdxscholar, P., Eisen, A., Smith, N., & Griesar, W. (2018). Exploration of Ayahuasca's Mechanisms in the Exploration of Ayahuasca's Mechanisms in the Treatment of Stimulant Use Disorder Treatment of Stimulant Use Disorder.

Perkins, D., Opaleye, E. S., Simonova, H., Bouso, J. C., Tófoli, L. F., GalvÃo-Coelho, N. L., Schubert, V., & Sarris, J. (2021). Associations between ayahuasca consumption in naturalistic settings and current alcohol and drug use: Results of a large international cross-sectional survey. Drug and Alcohol Review, 41(1), 265–274.

Perkins, D., Schubert, V., Simonová, H., Tófoli, L. F., Bouso, J. C., Horák, M., Galvão-Coelho, N. L., & Sarris, J. (2021). Influence of Context and Setting on the Mental Health and Wellbeing Outcomes of Ayahuasca Drinkers: Results of a Large International Survey. Frontiers in Pharmacology, 12.

Prueger, S. (2021, April 23). Ibogaine Providers: How A Medical Subculture Changed the World. Psychable.

Rootman, J. M., Kryskow, P., Harvey, K., Stamets, P., Santos-Brault, E., Kuypers, K. P. C., Polito, V., Bourzat, F., & Walsh, Z. (2021). Adults who microdose psychedelics report health related motivations and lower levels of anxiety and depression compared to non-microdosers. Scientific Reports, 11(1), 22479.

Sarris, J., Perkins, D., Cribb, L., Schubert, V., Opaleye, E., Bouso, J. C., Scheidegger, M., Aicher, H., Simonova, H., Horák, M., Galvão-Coelho, N. L., Castle, D., & Tófoli, L. F. (2021). Ayahuasca use and reported effects on depression and anxiety symptoms: An international cross-sectional study of 11,912 consumers. Journal of Affective Disorders Reports, 4, 100098.

Savinelli, A., & Halpern, J. H. (1995, August 1). MAPS - MAOI

Contraindications [related to Ayahuasca]. Maps.org.

Savoldi, R., Polari, D., Pinheiro-da-Silva, J., Silva, P. F., Lobao-Soares, B., Yonamine, M., Freire, F. A. M., & Luchiari, A. C. (2017). Behavioral Changes Over Time Following Ayahuasca Exposure in Zebrafish. Frontiers in Behavioral Neuroscience, 11.

Shpongle. (2005). Shpongle - Nothing Lasts... But Nothing Is Lost. Www.discogs.com.

Shulgin, A., & Shulgin, A. (1997). Tihkal: The Continuation.. Transform Press.

Turek, J. (2020). Jan Turek: Archaeology of Death, 8 - Shamanism and burials in the Palaeolithic period. Department of Archaeology, Charles University, Prague.

Uthaug, M. V., van Oorsouw, K., Kuypers, K. P. C., van Boxtel, M., Broers, N. J., Mason, N. L., Toennes, S. W., Riba, J., & Ramaekers, J. G. (2018). Sub-acute and long-term effects of ayahuasca on affect and cognitive thinking style and their association with ego dissolution. Psychopharmacology, 235(10), 2979–2989.

VanPool, C. S. (2009). The signs of the sacred: Identifying shamans using archaeological evidence. Journal of Anthropological Archaeology, 28(2), 177–190.

Virdi, J. (2020, October 26). Reexamining Cultural Beliefs Around Children and Psychedelics. Psychedelics Today.

Wolff, T. J. (2020). The Touristic Use of Ayahuasca in Peru: Expectations, Experiences, Meanings and Subjective Effects. Springer Nature.

Other Books By Sofia Visconti

Available now in Ebook, Paperback, Hardcover, and Audiobook in all regions.

www.ingramcontent.com/pod-product-compliance
Lightning Source LLC
Chambersburg PA
CBHW050237120526
44590CB00016B/2127